Macroeconomics from the Bottom-up

New Economic Windows

Domenico Delli Gatti · Saul Desiderio
Edoardo Gaffeo · Pasquale Cirillo
Mauro Gallegati

Macroeconomics from the Bottom-up

Springer

Domenico Delli Gatti
Catholic University of Milan, Italy

Saul Desiderio
Università Politecnica delle Marche, Ancona, Italy

Edoardo Gaffeo
University of Trento, Italy

Pasquale Cirillo
University of Bern, Switzerland

Mauro Gallegati
Università Politecnica delle Marche, Ancona, Italy

New Economic Windows
ISSN print edition: 2039-411X
ISSN electronic edition: 2039-4128

ISBN 978-88-470-1970-6
ISBN 978-88-470-1971-3 (eBook)
DOI 10.1007/978-88-470-1971-3

Springer Milan Dordrecht Heidelberg London New York

Library of Congress Control Number: 2011921275

Cover design: Simona Colombo, Milano
Typesetting: le-tex publishing services GmbH, Leipzig, Germany

Printed on acid-free paper

Springer-Verlag Italia S.r.l., Via Decembrio 28, I-20137 Milano
Springer is part of Springer Science+Business Media (www.springer.com)

To Hy Minsky,

who strived to teach us how to get involved with
non-speculative (no-Ponzi) economic research,
and how ridiculous economic theorems can be
when they are detached from the real world

Preface and Acknowledgements

The ideas and results in this book represent the culmination of a research project aimed at exploring macroeconomic issues moving from premises alternative to those employed by the current mainstream. The nickname informally assigned to the project – *CATS* – was originally chosen to honour two members of the research group (DDG and MG), as that was the way the lamented Hyman Minsky once baptised them because of an allegedly common zoological root in their family names. After joking on it for some time we realized that *CATS* could also perfectly summarize the deep-rooted methodology inspiring our approach, according to which any economy – and, *a fortiori*, a large industrialized macro-economy – should be modelled as a ***C****omplex* ***A****dap****T****ive* ***S****ystem* to be analyzed by means of agent-based computational experiments.

The bulk of us (DDG, EG, MG) has already offered a first introduction to the potentialities of an agent-based approach to macroeconomics in another book, *Emergent Macroeconomics* (EM) (Delli Gatti *et al.*, 2008). This new endeavour is partly a follow up, and partly an upgrading. In fact, analogously to EM the key idea we maintain and develop throughout this book is that theoretical representations of macroeconomic phenomena cannot be inferred from the fully predetermined behaviour of a representative agent, whose actions bring him unfailingly to an equilibrium, thanks to the hidden coordinating guide of the Walrasian auctioneer. In contrast to this view, we do believe that a theory of macroeconomic outcomes should be explained as emerging from the continuous *adaptive dispersed interactions* of a multitude of *autonomous, heterogeneous and bounded rational agents* living in a *truly uncertain environment*.

Differently from EM, however, in the framework we shall present in what follows *all* the aggregate variables (price and wage indices, quantities supplied and demanded, interest rates) are endogenously determined through completely decentralized trades. Agents acts purposively to discover their *right* individual ask/bid prices and offer/demand quantities, that is the prices and quantities which sometimes clear the small portions of market in which they happen to operate. However, none of them is interested in the properties of the economy as a whole, let alone in knowing if the system admits a unique and stable aggregate equilibrium. None of them is asked to solve astonishingly difficult optimization problems, simply because the presence of endogenous uncertainty makes such an effort completely unaffordable. On these premises, we build a computational laboratory which allows us to provide a *general* (i.e., multi-market) description of how a macroeconomy evolves in time, but also to keep track of the artificial history of each single agent. In addition to the results we were able to obtain with the approach followed in EM, we are now in a position to address a wider range of typical macroeconomic issues, such as the relationship among output growth, productivity and inflation, or the emergence of wage-price spirals.

As any culmination should be, we hope this book will represent a new start also. Some hints on possible directions for future investigations will be offered in the final chapter. What is more, we look forward to seeing the development and maturity of a "agent-based-macro" community of scholars, focused deeply on the view according to which "[…] the economy is best conceived of as a network of interacting processors, each one with less capacity to process information than would be required of a central processor set to solve the overall allocation problem for the entire system" (Leijonhuvfud, 1993). Should this volume contribute a few steps along this perilous but exciting route, our mission would be accomplished.

In this volume we present a lot of unpublished material developed during the last four years, especially regarding the methodological underpinnings of our approach, the sensitivity analysis of the model and validation exercises. The rest derives from articles we have published in the meantime, as "Complex agent-based macroeconomics: a manifesto for a new paradigm" (2010, *Journal of Economic Interaction and Coordination*), "Adaptive microfoundations for emergent macroeconomics" (2008, *Eastern Economic Journal*) and "Reflections on modern macroeconomics: can we travel along a safer road?" (2007, *Physica A*).

The list of people who deserve our thanks for their help during the preparation of this book is very long. At different stages of the *CATS* adventure, we were fortunate enough in profiting from the excellent teamwork secured by Tiziana Assenza, Leonardo Bargigli, Stefano Battiston, Michele Catalano, Fabio Clementi, Giulia De Masi, Corrado Di Guilmi, Marco Gallegati, Gianfranco Giulioni, Umberto Gostoli, Mauro Napoletano, Eniel Ninka, Antonio Palestrini, Matteo Richiardi, Alberto Russo, Emiliano Santoro and Gabriele Tedeschi. Somehow, all of them should be considered accomplices for the product in front of you, in ways perhaps they do not fully recognize. But we do.

We owe a huge intellectual debt (and several dinners) to Bruce Greenwald and Joe Stiglitz, who hosted us at Columbia University many times. The thought-provoking discussions we had with them stimulated and sustained the development of our thinking on this subject. The vision outlined in this work has been also sensibly refined in the course of stimulating conversations with many EURACE friends, in particular Silvano Cincotti and Herbert Dawid.

Many thanks are due to Mario Amendola, Robert Axtell, Buzz Brock, Carl Chiarella, Giovanni Dosi, Giorgio Fagiolo, Piero Ferri, Peter Flaschel, Duncan Foley, Cars Hommes, Alan Kirman, Blake LeBaron, Marco Lippi, Thomas Lux,

Luciano Pietronero, James Ramsey, Barkley Rosser *Jr.*, Willi Semmler, Roberto Tamborini, Leanne Ussher and several anonymous referees for many useful comments to the *CATS* papers and/or to an early version of this manuscript. Although undoubtedly none of them will be completely satisfied with the final result, we can guarantee it would have been much worse without their effort, patience, competence and friendship. Furthermore, comments and suggestions from participants in many presentations held at several conferences, institutes and universities [WEHIA06-08-09 (Bologna-Warsaw-Beijing); Eastern Economic Association Conference 2007 (New York); Società Italiana degli Economisti Conference 2007 (Turin); International Conference on Complex Systems 2008 (Hebrew-Jerusalem); Econophysics Colloquia at Ancona, Kolkata, Tokyo and Turin; ISI Foundation, Turin; ICSIM, Villalago; ATR Laboratories, Kyoto; Ettore Majorana Center, Erice; Bielefield, Lecce, Lille, Milano "Cattolica", Paris 2, Porto Alegre, Roma "La Sapienza", Siena, Turin, Trento] helped us very much.

The research leading to these results has received financial support from the Italian Ministry of Research (PRIN06-08), the European Community's Sixth [FP6 (EURACE)] and Seventh [FP7 (POLHIA, FINNOV (grant agreement n° 217466))] Framework Programmes, the Universities Catholic of Milan, UPM and Trento, and the Autonomous Province of Trento. We gratefully acknowledge all these Institutions for their generosity.

Milan, January 2011

Domenico Delli Gatti
Saul Desiderio
Edoardo Gaffeo
Pasquale Cirillo
Mauro Gallegati

Contents

Chapter 1
Introducing *Bottom-up Adaptive Macroeconomics*

> People are responding to an environment that consists of other people responding to *their* environment, which consists of people responding to an environment of people's responses. Sometimes the dynamics are sequential … Sometimes the dynamics are reciprocal … These situations, in which people's behaviour or people's choices depend on the behaviour or the choices of other people, are the ones that usually don't permit any simple summation or extrapolation to the aggregates. To make that connection we usually have to look at the *system of interaction* between individuals and their environment.
>
> THOMAS C. SCHELLING
> *Micromotives and Macrobehavior*, p. 14

1.1 At the Roots of the Mainstream *Weltanschauung*

Contemporary economics is in troubled waters. This is true most of all for that particular area of the economic discourse labeled macroeconomics. Although in our days there exists a consolidated and celebrated mainstream framework known as Dynamic Stochastic General Equilibrium (DSGE) model (Blanchard, 2008; Woodford, 2008), its internal coherence and ability in explaining the empirical evidence are increasingly questioned from several quarters (Colander, 2006; Howitt *et al.*, 2008; Juselius and Franchi, 2007), especially after the turmoil of the first global crises of the XXIst century has materialized almost unannounced and misconstrued (Driffill, 2008).

Maybe surprisingly, the causes of the present state of affairs go back at least to the mid of the eighteenth century, when some of the Western economies were twisted by the technological and institutional advancements which led to the industrial revolution, and the new-born *political economy* was still a small portion of moral philosophy striving for disciplinary autonomy. This happened roughly one century after the Newtonian revolution re-founded physics on new grounds: from the small apple to the enormous planets, all physical objects were found to eventually obey the simple *natural* and *deterministic* law of universal gravitation. It was therefore natural for the then emancipating figure of social scientist (*the economist*) to increasingly borrow the method (*mathematics*) of the most successful and admired among the hard sciences (*physics*), allowing for the mutation of political economy into *economics*. In the end, it was the mechanical physics of the seventeen century which inspired the marginalist revolution of the 1870s leaded by Stanley Jevons, Carl Menger and Leon Walras: any explanation of human behavior must be necessarily brought back to that of a selfish *Homo Oeconomicus*, who makes axiomatic-defined rational calculations aimed at maximizing a context-independent utility function.[1] From then on – precisely while in many other domains of human knowledge it was becoming clear that the mechanical model could no longer be considered as universal – economics started to live its own placid disciplinary evolution firmly rooted on the holy trinity of classical physics, i.e. reductionism, determinism and mechanicism.

Quite remarkably, it must be admitted that the probabilistic approach of relativity theory and statistical physics, which deeply shook the foundations of physical sciences at the turn of the nineteenth century, found their authoritative counterparts also in economics during the two decades of *the high theory* (i.e. the 1920s and the 1930s).[2] In two independent contributions published in the same year, Frank H. Knight and John Maynard Keynes made forcefully the point that economic decisions are usually taken in circumstances of radical uncertainty, in which probability statements cannot be deemed as absolute – that is, given once and for all – nor comparable (Knight, 1921; Keynes, 1921). On the contrary, the notion of probability – and, as a consequence, of expectation – is fundamentally relative:

> No proposition is in itself either probable or improbable, just as no place can be intrinsically distant; and the probability of the same statement varies with the evidence presented, which is, as it were, its origin of reference. (Keynes, 1921, p. 7)

Albeit largely unnoticed by many of his numerous exegetists, Keynes was largely inspired by relativistic ideas also in his more famous *General Theory* (Keynes, 1936). In this respect, two basic claims can be advanced (Togati, 2001). First, he made a clear distinction between the analysis of individual behavior and that of macroeconomic aggregates, which paralleled the dismissing of atomism and the

[1] In the final chapter of his *General Theory*, Keynes (1936) wrote of contemporaneous politicians as intellectual slaves of economists passed away at least a decade before. Extending this metaphor, XXI century economists are intellectual slaves of the mummified physicists of the XVII century (see also Mirowski, 1989).

[2] Phelps (1990) inserts the uprising of the probabilistic approach in economics into the wider intellectual revolution known as *modernism*, a cultural and philosophical approach which transformed the Western world between 1860 and 1930, and that comprises "… the cubism of Picasso and Braque, the atonalism of Schoenberg and Berg, the fragmented poetry of Eliot and Pound, and various writings from Nietzsche to Sartre" (Phelps, 1990, p. 5).

introduction of the concept of field made a few years before by Albert Einstein. In Keynes' words:

> The right dichotomy is, I suggest, between the theory of the individual industry or firm [...] on the one hand, and the theory of output and employment *as a whole* on the other one. (Keynes, 1936, p. 293; emphasis in original)

What Keynes argued is that macroeconomic aggregates can be explained if and only if individuals are studied by recurring to a systemic perspective, according to which conventional factors – themselves the unintended products of agents' interactions – instruct and constrain individual behaviors and expectations. Second, in line with the rejection of absolute time and space carried out in modern physics by Einstein, Keynes maintained that conventions – far from being given once for all – are inherently time-contingent. The counterpart of Einstenian Relativism in Keynesian economics was the explicit acknowledgment that in general agents take decisions by following conventional rules of conduct in conditions of radical uncertainty, and that from time to time the prevailing convention abruptly breaks down:

> It is not surprising that a convention, in an absolute view of things so arbitrary, should have its weak points. [...] A conventional valuation which is established as the outcome of the mass psychology of a large number of ignorant individuals is liable to change violently as the result of sudden fluctuations of opinion due to factors which do not really make much difference to the prospective yield, since there will be no strong roots to hold it steady. [...] In abnormal times, the market will be subject to waves of optimistic and pessimistic sentiment. (Keynes, 1936, pp. 153–4)

This does not necessarily imply that agents' behavior should be seen as irrational, nor that some regularity in economic life cannot be detected. On the contrary, different circumstances call for different criteria of individual rationality: in some cases maximization is feasible and practicable, in some others routinized behavior constitutes a best response. Furthermore, while an external observer cannot fully predetermine the causal mechanism that drives individual behavior and market outcomes under those different circumstances, qualitative restrictions on probabilistic representations of change can be used to fruitfully distinguish between alternative explanations of empirical outcomes.

In spite of the exceptional success of its practical implementation during the two decades following the end of the IInd World War, however, the theoretical underpinnings of the Keynesian revolution has been never fully grasped inside the profession. This became manifest at the turn of the 1960s, when the neoclassical counter-revolution framed backed the discipline into the traditional marginalist approach and ignored almost by definition any interdependence among agents on the one hand, and any difference between individual and aggregate behavior on the other one. The ideas of natural laws, equilibrium theory and a unified structure of explanation was re-inserted into the theoretical *corpus* of pre-Keynesian economics *sic et simpliciter*, and their combination with rational expectations gave rise to a paradigm which has flourished to our days as the winning one. In such a setting, the relationship between individuals and aggregates can again be analyzed under a strict reductionist approach. Aggregation is thus simply the process of summing up the market outcomes of individual entities, in order to obtain economy-wide totals. In other words, contemporary models postulate that there is not any significant difference between microeconomics and macroeconomics: the dynamics of the whole is nothing but a summation of the dynamics of its components.

The trouble with the mainstream approach is that it uses a methodological approach – namely *logical empiricism*, according to which all statements should be testable, even if they are the product of theories which have elements with no empirical counterparts[3] – which has proved to be so weak in its assumptions and so dogmatic in its evolution to have been repeatedly ridiculed by arrays of epistemologists (Caldwell, 1993). Economists also have made their part in denouncing this state of affair. The radical constructionist approach centered on the use of representative agencies to be associated with per-capita empirical data, for instance, has been shown to be theoretically and empirically inconsistent unless a battery of widely implausible restrictions hold true (Kirman, 1992; Forni and Lippi, 1998). The notion of Walrasian general equilibrium is another dramatic example (Ackerman, 2002). In many economic models, the equilibrium is customarily described as a state of rest in which demand exactly equals supply, both at the individual and at the aggregate levels, but where not every individual agent or market – read, the *Walrasian auctioneer* – is described. This representation is instrumental to a theory aimed at explaining how given goods and productive inputs are (or should be) efficiently allocated among alternative ends. This does not come for free, however. In fact, an allocation can be (Pareto) optimal if and only if one is willing to expunge from the picture any kind of externality (increasing returns due to division of labor, non-price interactions, interdependencies in expectation formation, etc.) and to allow information to be complete, as the First Welfare Theorem implicitly shows.

We argue that a mechanical extension to economic phenomena of the limited concept of static equilibrium developed in classical mechanics has been at one time unfortunate and unnecessary. On the contrary, taking stock of the evolution of ideas occurred in those same disciplines which originally inspired economics as a science might have proven extremely useful. This point has been authoratively made before. In the preface to his *Principles*, for instance, Alfred Marshall vaticinated that *the Mecca of the economist lies in economic biology rather than in economic dynamics* (Marshall, 1961, p. *xiv*). What he meant was that, since economics deals with humans striving to learn how (metaphorically or not) to survive in a competitive environment, evolution and structural irreversible change are the *granum salis* of real economies, and they must represent the key subjects of any

[3] This is the case for the well-known *as if* argument put forth by Friedman (1953), according to which the primary appraisal criterion of a theory should be its predictive success, and not the truth content of its assumptions.

theory aimed at explaining them. A proper account of irreversibility, for instance, implies that the possibility to default because of tragic errors or fatal accidents should be a key ingredient of the model.

Unfortunately, Marshall himself failed to go beyond a mere enunciation of principles, and he undauntedly continued to make use of a mechanicistic *partial equilibrium* approach in his scientific endeavour, with the exception of a single chapter devoted to industrial organization (Hodgson, 1993). His methodological legacy is still alive and kicking today. Going back to the issue of how to model default risk in macroeconomics, it is almost tautological to assert that DSGE models are structurally unable to deal with it: let your representative agent go bankrupt, and the whole story ends.

In fact, an explicit analysis of economic change requires concepts and methods largely unfamiliar to contemporary neoclassical economics, but that have long been available in other disciplines acquainted to deal with dynamics in real time. Scholars interested in the sociology of economics could probably try to explain why post-graduate students in economics are still now largely unexposed to these concepts. But the fact remains. As a matter of example, the notion of *statistical equilibrium*, in which the aggregate equilibrium is compatible with individual disequilibrium, is outside the toolbox of the average mainstream economist.[4] The same is largely true for the notion of *evolutionary equilibrium* (at an aggregate level) and *punctuated equilibrium* developed in evolutionary biology.[5] The issue of *aggregation* is a final point in case. What contemporary macroeconomists typically fail to realize is that in studying the complex dance of heterogeneous motivations, behaviors and beliefs characterizing a real modern economy, the correct procedure of aggregation is not just the *per-capita* expected value; with heterogeneity and interaction higher moments enter the scene, and their dynamics must be seriously taken into account (Stocker, 1984; Gallegati *et al.*, 2006). Furthermore, methodological individualism must be enriched with the introduction of levels of analysis above the individual, like group selection (Bergstrom, 2001). Mainstream macroeconomic models do not take into consideration that there might be two-way interdependencies between individuals and aggregates: interacting elements produce aggregate patterns to which those individuals in turn react to. This is precisely where the concept of *emergence* enters the picture.

As in Epstein and Axtell (1996), in this book we employ the term *emergence* to simply characterize the arising of stable and orderly aggregate structures from simple adaptive individual rules of conduct.[6] Loosely stated, we shall argue to be

[4] The interested reader is referred to the pioneering work of Duncan Foley (Foley, 1994; 1996) and Masanao Aoki (1996; 2000).

[5] Illuminating enough, for evolutionary biologists an organism reaches a state of rest (i.e., an equilibrium, according to mainstream economics) only when it is dead.

[6] We resist the pretension to a more precise definition for the simple reasons that the term itself – and its counterpart *complexity*, to which we will come in due course – is one or the most slippery in the recent history of science (Israel, 2005), and its antecedents are dreadfully connected to non-scientific argumentations (Epstein, 1999).

in the presence of an emergent phenomenon whenever the whole ensemble achieves functionalities or properties which its constituent parts – if taken in isolation – lack. Exemplifying from the physical world, ice and steam are emergent properties of water as they are properties of how water molecules are collectively aligned, not of one molecule in isolation. Since we are ultimately interested in *explaining* empirical facts, however, any emergent phenomena must be deducible – or, to use the language of Epstein (1999), must be *generable* – from a description of elementary elements and – here is the novelty – their interactions. Of the three entities composing the holy trinity of physicists' *Pantheon*, therefore, at least one seems in some sense inescapable, namely reductionism, if only because any attempt at explanation inevitably implies some form of *reduction* or simplification of reality (Epstein, 2007; Israel, 2005). This point is critical, and it deservers a clarification. What must be refused is not reductionism per se, that is the idea that to understand a complex system we need an adequate description of the individual characteristics and of the network of interactions of its constituents, but *methodological reductionism* in its strongest form, according to which "the whole is simply the sum of the parts".[7] On the contrary, in a complex system the whole constitutes something which is *more and different* than the mere linear combination of its constitutive parts. Even if we are able to know the fundamentals of all the components of a particular system (low-level description), that knowledge by itself is not sufficient to fully reconstruct the characteristics of the system (high-level description). Paul Anderson (1972) admirably illustrates the point:

> The reductionist hypothesis does not by any means imply a "constructionist" one: The ability to reduce everything to simple fundamental laws does not imply the ability to start from those laws and reconstruct the universe. [...] The constructionist hypothesis breaks down when confronted with the twin difficulties of scale and complexity. The behavior of large and complex aggregates of elementary particles, it turns out, is not to be understood in terms of a simple extrapolation of the properties of a few particles. Instead, at each level of complexity new properties appear. [...] At each stage entirely new laws, concepts and generalizations are necessary. [...] Psychology is not applied biology, nor is biology applied chemistry. (Anderson, 1972, p. 393)

Also in economics, a plethora of empirical evidence and experimental tests have persuasively demonstrated that aggregation generates identifiable regularities which can not be immediately conduced to the characteristics of individuals: simple individual rules, when aggregated, produce statistical regularities or well-shaped aggregate functions that cannot be derived from the behavior of individual entities taken in isolation. Härdel and Kirman (1995), for example, use figures on the Marseille fish market to show that individual data on market demand reveals none of the properties one would expect from standard theory. In spite of this, at the aggregate level standard downward-sloping demand curves emerge. Ariely *et al.* (2003), in turn, use experimental data to reinforce this result, showing how

[7] Methodological reductionism, that is the reduction of theories along a tree of knowledge (from socio-economics down to psychology, biology, chemistry and eventually physics), is referred also as *hierarchical reductionism* by Dawkins (1976).

coherent aggregate behavior estimated from market demand curve is consistent with arbitrary behavior at the individual level.

While Keynes admirably apprehended this truth and tried to transplant it into the economic discourse, mainstream macroeconomists have simply removed it altogether. We argue that a more insightful approach to macroeconomics should start from a reappraisal of such a tradition. Moving from the Keynes' lesson, the line of attack we propose starts from the idea that aggregate variables – like the GDP, the consumer price index or the unemployment rate, and aggregate psychological data like the propensity to consume or the liquidity preference – cannot be reduced to a sum of mutually consistent and rational individual decisions, but are the (largely) unintended product of the continuous interaction among a multitude of heterogeneous goal-seeking individuals. Put it in another way, regularities emerge from individual "chaos" (Lavoie, 1989).

Once again, an essential source of inspiration for discovering a plausible way out of the difficulties of the mainstream approach can be found in the contemporary evolution of biology and physics. There, the last three decades have witnessed a passage from a view emphasizing change in terms of finalized predetermined evolution to a view emphasizing *self-organized criticality*, according to which a system with many heterogeneous interacting agents reaches a statistical aggregate equilibrium characterized by the appearance of some (often scale free) steady distribution (Bak, 1997, Gould, 1996). These distributions are no longer "optimal" or "efficient" according to some welfare criterion: they are simply the natural outcome of individual interactions, in which both chance (novelty due to random circumstances) and necessity (predetermined conditions) play a peculiar role. Accordingly, in the models contained in this book, the equilibrium of a system no longer requires every single element to be in equilibrium by itself, but rather that the statistical distributions describing aggregate phenomena be stable, i.e. in "[...] a state of macroscopic equilibrium maintained by a large number of transitions in opposite directions" (Feller, 1957; p. 356). In other words, along a system equilibrium individual disequibria tend to offset each other, so that the aggregate system reaches endogenously an aggregate order of the type described by Hayek (1977).

1.2 Flawed Microfoundations for Irrelevant Macro?

During the last fifteen years, the field of macroeconomics has experienced a rapid convergence towards a commonly accepted paradigm, baptized as *new neoclassical synthesis* (NNS) (Goodfriend and King, 1997), whose most visible and fashionable outcome is the class of DSGE models.[8] Remarkably, macroeconomics models published in top-ranking academic journals look nowadays almost similar to each other in structure, regardless of the research question they address or the

8 See, among the others, Christiano *et al.* (2005) and Smets and Wouters (2003).

emphasis they put on theoretical versus empirical analysis. The main idea behind the NNS rests on the blending of key elements of neoclassical real business cycle theory with key elements of the new Keynesian tradition of the 1980s. A quick look at the contributions each one of them added to the synthesis should help us to put in perspective the pros and cons of the current state of macroeconomics.

The research program launched at the end of the 1970s by adherents to the new Classical school and the real business cycle (RBC) approach was centered on a simple but far-reaching idea: in order to evaluate within a single and consistent framework issues related to either short-run fluctuations and long-run growth, structural macroeconomic models should be firmly rooted on intertemporal general equilibrium (GE) foundations. In the words of Robert Lucas and Tom Sargent:

> An economy following a multivariate stochastic process is now routinely described as being in equilibrium, by which is meant nothing more that at each point in time (a) markets clears and (b) agents act in their own self-interest. This development, which stemmed mainly from the work of Arrow [...] and Debreu [...], implies that simply to look at any economic time series and conclude that it is a disequilibrium phenomenon is a meaningless observation. [...] The key elements of these models are that agents are rational, reacting to policy changes in a way which is in their best interests privately, and that the impulses which trigger business fluctuations are mainly unanticipated shocks. (Lucas and Sargent, 1978, p. 7)

A natural by-product of this approach is that microeconomic and macroeconomic analysis should no longer be seen to involve fundamentally different principles. Theoretical statements about household or firm behavior, as well as theoretical statements about the functioning of individual markets, can be immediately reconciled with a model of the aggregate economy:

> The most interesting recent developments in macroeconomic theory seem to me describable as the reincorporation of aggregative problems [...] within the general framework of "microeconomic" theory. If these developments succeed, the term "macroeconomic" will be simply disappear from use and the modifier "micro" will become superfluous. We will simply speak, as did Smith, Marshall and Walras, of *economic theory*.[9] (Lucas, 1987, pp. 107–8)

According to this view, economic phenomena at a macroscopic level can be modeled – hence, *explained* – as a weighted sum of the equilibrium market outcomes of homogeneous individual decision makers,[10] so that the per-capita dynamic behavior of the aggregate is identical to that of a single microeconomic agent. The analytical cornerstone to reach this result consists in refurbishing the competitive

---

[9] Even if we doubt that Smith, Marshall and Walras would have embraced the idea of *economic theory* that Lucas has in mind.

[10] It seems worthwhile to notice that this procedure of microfoundation of macroeconomics is very different from the methodological counterpart used in physics. The latter starts from the micro-dynamics of the single particle, as expressed by the Liouville equation and, through the Master equation, ends up with macroscopic equations. In the aggregation process, the dynamics of the individual entities lose their degree of freedom and behaves coherently in the aggregate.

GE model elaborated in the 1870s by Leon Walras, that is a configuration of prices and plans of action such that, at those prices, all agents can carry out their chosen plans and, consequently, all markets clear. Real business cycle economists[11] recurred, in particular, to the refinement proposed in the 1950s by Arrow and Debreu (1954), who showed that also individual intertemporal (on an infinite horizon) optimization yields a GE, as soon as the economy is equipped with perfect price foresights for each future state of nature and a complete set of Arrow-securities markets (Arrow, 1964), all open at time zero and closed simultaneously. Whenever these conditions hold true, the GE is an allocation that maximizes a properly defined social welfare function, or the equilibrium is Pareto-efficient (*First Welfare Theorem*).

At odds with RBC theorists, who insisted in ethereal parables built on models with perfectly competitive equilibria, the counterpart involved in the NNS – i.e. new Keynesians (NEKs) – moved from facts, whose power is hard to ignore in the long-run. Among them, one is really remarkable. Shifts in aggregate demand, due for example to unexpected monetary policy, affect output substantially more than would be expected in an economy with perfectly flexible prices and wages. The line of attack chosen by NEKs consisted in accepting the methodological glove threw down by RBC theorists, showing that real and nominal rigidities – responsible in the end of the *excess sensitivity* of output to demand shocks – can be derived from first principles on the one hand, and that a variety of types of adjustment frictions can be easily incorporated into dynamic GE models on the other one. A large literature has stressed that this re-interpretation of Keynes' ideas has almost nothing to do with what Keynes' himself thought about how a dynamic market economy really works. But this criticisms has been largely considered by mainstream macroeconomists as a nuisance.

Summarizing, in its basic incarnation the NNS-DSGE model which is currently monopolizing macroeconomics is a dynamic (i.e., infinite horizon), rational-expectation GE model with two imperfections added: *i*) monopolistic competition in the goods market; and *ii*) a deterministic (*à la* Taylor) or stochastic (*à la* Calvo) time-dependent price-setting rule. While the mathematics required to solve the model may at times look tricky and intimidating,[12] conceptually the model is disappointingly unrefined: starting from a discounted sum of infinite utilities and an intertemporal budget constraint, somewhere you will eventually find a marginal rate of substitution equating a relative price, and possibly an additional binding constraint that prevents the second-best from being achieved. Nothing is said about true heterogeneity in preferences and beliefs; the behavior of agents along disequilibrium paths; the net of non-market interactions linking agents; the insur-

[11] The classical references are Kydland and Prescott (1982), and Long and Plosser (1983).

[12] Form this viewpoint, modern macroeconomists have provided an unambiguous answer to the question that Marshall posed when commenting a cornerstone of marginalism, that is *Mathematical Psychics* by F.Y. Edgeworth: "It will be interesting to watch the development of his theory, and, in particular, to see how far he succeeds in preventing his mathematics from running away with him, and carrying him out of sight of the actual facts of economics" (Marshall, 1881, p. 457).

gence of intratemporal and intertemporal coordination problems; in a nutshell, nothing is said about what really makes any macroeconomic system an object worth studying.

The logical inconsistencies of the mainstream NNS approach have been pointed out by a large, albeit dispersed, literature.[13] A brief discussion of the points we believe are the most relevant seems worthwhile.

The SDM result. It is well known that the GE is neither unique nor locally stable under general conditions. This negative result, which refers to the work of Sonnenschein (1972), Debreu (1974) and Mantel (1974) – from hereafter, the SDM result – can be summarized along the following lines. Let the aggregate excess demand function $F(p)$ – obtained from aggregating among individual excess demands $f(p)$ – be a mapping from the price simplex Π to the commodity space P^N. A GE is defined as a price vector p such that $F(p^*)=0$. It turns out that the only conditions that $F(\cdot)$ inherits from $f(\cdot)$ are continuity, homogeneity of degree zero and the Walras' law (i.e., the total value of excess demand is zero). These assure the existence, but neither the uniqueness nor the local stability of p^*, unless preferences generating individual demand functions are restricted to very implausible cases.[14] For a theory which claims to be rooted on *general* equilibrium, the simple fact that general conclusions could be drawn for specific examples only represents a reversal of ordinary logic.

The RA hypothesis. A possible way out of the SDM result – one which has been adopted acritically and massively by NNS macroeconomists – consists in founding the analysis on a fictitious representative agent (RA) (Kirman, 1992). According to this approach, aggregate consumption is analyzed as if it were the consumption of a single individual, who frequently lives forever, while economy-wide substitution and income effects are restricted to coincide with that of the RA. Similarly, the labor market and the financial market are treated as a single worker and investor, respectively. Unfortunately, as Hildenbrand and Kirman (1988) note:

> There are no assumptions on isolated individuals, which will give us the properties of aggregate behavior. We are reduced to making assumptions at the aggregate level, which cannot be justified, by the usual individualistic assumptions. This problem is usually avoided in the macroeconomic literature by assuming that the economy behaves like an individual. Such an assumption cannot be justified in the context of the standard model. (Hildebrand and Kirman, 1988, p. 239)

[13] Davis (2006) identifies three "impossibility results" at the root of the breakdown of neoclassical economics and, by extension, of the NNS: (*i*) Arrow's impossibility theorem, showing that neoclassical theory is unable to explain social choices (Arrow, 1951); (*ii*) the Cambridge capital debate, pointing out that neoclassical economics is contradictory with respect to the concept of aggregate capital (Cohen and Harcourt, 2003); and (*iii*) the Sonnenschein-Debreu-Mantel result, showing that the standard comparative static reasoning is inapplicable in general equilibrium models. In the main text we limit ourselves to discuss several declensions of the latter point.

[14] For instance, one might require that all agents in the economy have Cobb-Douglas preferences.

Even when the model allows for heterogeneity, non-market interactions (that is, interactions not mediated by the price vector) are generally ruled out, and the so-called *weak interaction hypothesis* is invoked (Rios Rull, 1995).

Computability of a GE. The existence of a GE is customarily proved *via* the Brower's fix point theorem, i.e. by finding a continuous function $g(\cdot) : \Pi \rightarrow \Pi$ so that any fix point for $g(\cdot)$ is also an equilibrium price vector $F(p^*)=0$. Suppose that we are interested in finding an algorithm, which, starting from an arbitrary price vector p, chooses price sequences to check for p^* and halts when it finds it. In other terms, to find the GE price vector $F(p^*)=0$ means that halting configurations are decidable. As this violates the undecidability of the halting problem for Turing Machines, from a recursion theoretic viewpoint the GE solution is incomputable (Richter and Wong, 1999; Velupillai, 2000). Notice that the same problem applies, in spite of its name, to the class of Computable GE models (Velupillai, 2005).

Price mechanisms. By construction, in a GE all transactions are undertaken at the same equilibrium price vector. Economic theory has worked out two mechanisms capable of reaching this outcome. First, one can assume that buyers and sellers adjust, costless, their optimal supplies and demands to prices called out by a (explicit or implicit) fictitious auctioneer, who continues to do his job until he finds a price vector which clears all markets. Only then transactions take place (Walras' assumption). Alternatively, buyers and sellers sign provisional contracts and are allowed to freely (i.e., without any cost) recontract until a price vector is found which makes individual plans fully compatible. Once again, transactions occur only after the equilibrium price vector has been established (Edgeworth's assumption). Regardless of the mechanism one adopts, the GE model is one in which the formation of prices precedes the process of exchange, instead of being the result of it, through a *tatonnement* process occurring in a meta-time. Real markets work the other way round and operates in real time, so that the GE model cannot be considered a scientific explanation of real economic phenomena (Arrow, 1959). But even if we assume that a realistic method of price adjustment in real time could be devised, an additional point links the issue of iterative price adjustment mechanisms to that of computability analyzed before. As shown in Saari and Simon (1978) and Saari (1985), any price adjustment process which possesses the ability to converge to a GE requires an infinite amount of information. Let an iterative price adjustment mechanism, such that current prices are a differentiable function of past excess demand and its partial derivative. Suppose now that there exists an upper bound on the amount of information to be used in the adjustment process, measured in terms of the number of past periods and the number of partial derivatives of the excess demand function one is allowed to use in adjusting prices. Then, it can be shown that there exists a mathematically robust number of cases for which convergence to the GE does not occur.[15]

[15] That is, cases of nonconvergence towards the GE occur on open sets of initial conditions, not just at isolated points.

Money. It has been widely recognized since Debreu (1959), that integrating money in the theory of value represented by the GE model is at best problematic. No economic agent can individually decide to monetize alone; monetary trade should be the equilibrium outcome of market interactions among optimizing agents. The use of money – that is, a common medium of exchange and a store of value – implies that one party to a transaction gives up something valuable (for instance, his endowment or production) for something inherently useless (a fiduciary token for which he has no immediate use) in the hope of advantageously re-trading it in the future. Given that in a GE model actual transactions take place only after a price vector coordinating all trading plans has been freely found, money can be consistently introduced into the picture only if the logical keystone of the absence of transaction costs is abandoned. By the same token, since credit makes sense only if agents can sign contracts in which one side promises future delivery of goods or services to the other side, in equilibrium markets for debt are meaningless, both information conditions and information processing requirements are not properly defined, and bankruptcy can be safely ignored. Finally, as the very notion of a GE implies that all transactions occur only when individual plans are mutually compatible, and this has to be true also in the labor market, the empirically observed phenomenon of involuntary unemployment and the microfoundation program put forth by Lucas, Sargent and their co-authors are logically inconsistent.

Time. The very absence of money and credit is a consequence of the fact that in GE there is no time. The only role assigned to time in a GE model is, in fact, that of dating commodities. Products, technologies and preferences are exogenously given and fixed from the outset. The convenient implication of banning out-of-equilibrium transactions is simply that of getting rid of any disturbing influence of intermediary modifications of endowments – and therefore of individual excess demands – on the final equilibrium outcome. The introduction of non-Walrasian elements into the GE microfoundations program – such as fixed or sticky prices, imperfect competition and incomplete markets leading to temporary equilibrium models – yields interesting Keynesian features such as the breaking of the Say's law and scope for a monetary theory of production, a rationale for financial institutions and a more persuasive treatment of informational frictions. As argued in Vriend (1994), however, all these approaches preserve a Walrasian perspective in that models are invariably closed by a GE solution concept, which, explicitly or (more often) not, implies the existence of a fictitious auctioneer who processes information, calculates equilibrium prices and quantities, and regulates transactions. As a result, if the Walrasian auctioneer is removed, the decentralized economy becomes dynamically incomplete, as we are not left with any mechanism determining how quantities and prices are set and how exchanges occur.

The macroeconomic equilibrium worked out by the RA is characterized by a complete absence of actual trades and verbal communications to exchange opinions with others. One must admit that this appears to be a rather counterfactual way to explain how a real economy works. However, it is not just what we miss as ingredients, but also what we loose from cooking the pudding in the wrong way that matters. In different contexts, Caballero (1992) and Gallegati (1993) show that RA models, by disregarding heterogeneity, non-convexities and direct interaction, abstract from stringent aggregation issues which inevitably lead the modeler to commit a fallacy of composition.[16] It would be quite easy to provide back-of-the-envelope examples in which a RA does not represent at all the individuals populating the economy, so that the reduction of a group of heterogeneous agents to an RA, far from being an innocuous analytical convenience, is "[...] both unjustified and leads to conclusions which are usually misleading and often wrong" (Kirman, 1992).

In addition to the logical drawbacks just discussed, macroeconomics built on the NNS inherited the methodological legacy of its neoclassical parent, in that it is axiomatic and based on unrealistic (and unverified) assumptions on purposeful human behavior. A well-known case in point is related to the rationality hypothesis, according to which not only a person's *entire* system of preferences and beliefs must be consistent with her actions, but also her beliefs about how the world works must hold true, at least on average (Vanberg, 2004). According to the supporters of NNS view, abstractions are necessary since the real world is complicated: far from compromising the epistemic contents of economics, the individual rationality hypothesis is essential for economic knowledge. After all, nobody really believes that economic agents are really unbounded rational. Though bounded rational by nature, however, people are forced by market evolutionary forces to learn optimal choices through practice, eventually acting *as if* they were fully rational. Admittedly, experimental evidence lends support to this position: repeated market experiences tend to facilitate the development of behavior consistent with rational choice theory (List and Millimet, 2008).

However, the *as if* argument does not invalidate the criticism of lack of realism we moved before, for at least two reasons. First, while the NNS requires internal coherence in order for theorems to be logically deduced from a set of assumptions, it abstracts from external coherence between theoretical statements and empirical evidence at the individual level: what experimental evidence shows is behavior consistent with *local* subjective rationality, where local refers to the consistency of preferences, beliefs and actions at the moment of choice.[17] Of course, this implies an important detachment from other more epistemologically robust falsifiable sciences (Rappaport, 1996). Second, learning rational behavior through market experience is possible whenever people are allowed to practice themselves in trading under stable circumstances, in an intelligible and predictable environment,

---

[16] In philosophy, the dual of the fallacy of composition is called *fallacy of division*, defined as the wrong practice of attributing properties to a level of analysis different than the one where the property is observed.

[17] Vanberg (2004) talks in this case of the *rationality postulate*, as opposed to the *rationality hypothesis*, which require *global* (i.e., complete) consistence of preferences, beliefs and actions.

and with small (or rapidly decreasing) deliberation costs at each repetition. Unfortunately, the research questions usually addressed in macroeconomics entail situations involving long and truly uncertain horizons – think at life cycle plans or at technological investments – and such a large number of degrees of freedom – for instance, how much does heterogeneity of consumers' and firms' balance sheet positions matter for the monetary transmission mechanism? – that are the least likely to meet the conditions for effective learning.

1.3 The ABC of Complex Economics

Are there other ways to *do* realistic (i.e., with individual rules of conduct and interaction structures being consistent with empirical observations) and useful (in guiding policymakers and in helping us to forecast) macroeconomic analysis beyond that inspired by the NNS-DSGE approach? In this book we argue for a positive answer. In particular, the solution we offer embrace the view that any economy –particularly, *large* economies composed of millions of individual entities – may and should be described as a complex, adaptive, dynamic system (Arthur *et al.*, 1997). Complexity arises because of the dispersed and non-linear interactions of a large number of heterogeneous autonomous agents. While we can naturally observe and measure macro outcomes – for instance, quantity and price indexes, as well as their growth rates – aggregates could not be deduced directly from an examination of the behavior of a *typical* individual in isolation. Global properties emerge instead from the market and non-market interactions of people without them being part of their intentions, a notion which clearly resembles the time-honored *invisible hand* metaphor advanced by Adam Smith.

Far from being an exotic novelty, in economics the complexity approach can boast a noble and long tradition. The history of economic thought of the last century is run through by a Karst river of heterodox theorizing whose leading roles, in one way or another, have contributed to design a coherent picture of adaptive humans undertaking dispersed interactions in decentralized markets under strong uncertainty. Beside the early influence of Frank Knight, John Maynard Keynes and Friedrich von Hayek, we are referring in particular to the ground-breaking work of towering figures like Armen Alchian, Axel Leijonhufvud, Thomas Schelling and Herbert Simon.

The shift of perspective brought in by a full comprehension of their lesson has two deep implications for macroeconomic theory. The first implication calls into question the rationality postulates usually advanced by mainstream economics to model human decision-making. By their very nature, optimization techniques guarantee the correspondence of substantive and procedural rationality if and only if all the consequences of alternative actions can be consistently conceived in advance, at least in a probabilistic sense. Unfortunately, for complex systems this possibility is generally ruled out, as interactive population dynamics gives rise to uncertainty that could not be reduced to risk in a Knightian sense[18] (Rosser, 2001). In turn, noncooperative game theory (Shubik, 1975) does not provide a way out under rather general conditions. Whenever players are heterogeneous as regards their strategy and information sets, a full adherence to strategic behavior modeling returns computationally complex problems, that is problems whose solution time (measured as the number of simple computational steps required to solve it) increases exponentially in the problem size. As the number of players increases – for large industrialized economies, the typical order of magnitude of agents acting on markets is 106 – the size of the problem is too large to complete a search for an optimal solution within a feasible time horizon. By its very nature, macroeconomics is a discipline concerning *large worlds* (Savage, 1954), that is situations in which economic agents do not possess well-defined models of the environment surrounding them. It turns out that as we shift attention from microeconomic scenarios to typical macroeconomic ones – that is, as we move from single market to multi-market parables – the very notion of rationality we can realistically ask to our models' characters should change. In large worlds, deductive means of reasoning are inapplicable or ill-defined; individuals instead build internal mental models and use heuristics to represent and interpret the world, learn from the outcomes of previous choices, and extrapolate from the particular to the general. Simply stated, agents must employ some form of induction (Arthur, 1992; Denzau and North, 1994).

In large interactive systems, individual decision processes become unavoidably adaptive, that is adjusted in the light of realized results, and the search for actions aimed at increasing individual performance stops as soon as a *satisficing* solution has been found (Simon, 1987). Adaptation is backward-looking, sequential and path-dependent. Desired prices, quantities, inventories, portfolio compositions, even the identity of whom we would like to trade are updated according to "error-correction" procedures. Expectations on the future course of events and results are clearly an important part of the decision-making process, but foresights are taken over finite horizons and are modified sequentially in the light of realized outcomes. While doing meaningful macroeconomics from a complex perspective, bounded rationality – both in terms of systematic reasoning errors and of costly deliberation activity – should be the rule, not the exception.

In complex economies, the key driver of evolution is not optimization but selection. Whenever the enforcement of contracts is costly and trades occur through face-to-face bargaining, maximizing behavior may yield lower payoffs than adherence to recognizable, forecastable social norms like reciprocity and cooperation (Schelling, 1978). Furthermore, Witt (1986) and Dutta and Radner (1999), among the others, have shown that the Friedmanesque *as if* argument to validating the profit maximization hypothesis – only firms whose managers maximize profits will survive in a competitive environment – does not hold even in more orthodox dynamical risky competitive models. In addition to sub-optimality at the individ-

[18] A possible way to define Knightian uncertainty is that the potential outcomes of an action are identified by two or more distributions at one time, and that these distributions are overlapping.

ual level, aggregate outcomes emerging from selection processes need not result in the efficient outcomes (Dew *et al.*, 2004). We shall come back later to this point. For the time being, it must be noticed that the essence of this argument were made by Alchian almost six decades ago:

> Realized positive profits, not maximum profits, are the mark of success and viability. [...] The pertinent requirement – positive profits through relative efficiency – is weaker than "maximized profits", with which, unfortunately, it has been confused. [...] The preceding interpretation suggests two ideas. First, success (survival) accompanies relative superiority; and, second, it does not require proper motivation but may rather be the result of fortuitous circumstances". (Alchian, 1950, p. 213)

The second implication of the complexity approach to macroeconomics deals with the common practice of *closing* models through the exogenous imposition of a general equilibrium solution by means of some fixed-point theorems. The introduction of a Walrasian auctioneer inhibits the researcher from exploring the real question at stake in macroeconomics, that is to explain how self-interested trading partners happen to coordinate themselves in decentralized markets most of the time, but also why from time to time some major economic disaster occurs without any apparent external cause. Complexity offers a way out of this situation, and it suggests new perspectives. Complex adaptive economies display a tendency to self-organize towards rather stable aggregate configurations, occasionally punctuated by bursts of rapid change. Spontaneous order emerges in the process of individual buying and selling transactions taking place in real space and time, without the need of any central controller. Adaptive and imitative behaviors give rise to stable and predictable aggregate configurations, as stability implies predictability and *vice versa*. Since it is sometimes safer to be wrong in the crowd than to be right alone, imbalances can now and then accumulate to the point that a bundle of chained bankruptcies becomes inevitable. After the bubble has burst and the system has experienced episodes of wild instability, new modes of adaptive behavior, technological opportunities and budget constraints co-evolve leading the economy towards a new phase of aggregate stability.

Readers acquainted with Austrian economics would had already recognized that the picture we have just drawn embraces the notion of *spontaneous market order* put forward by Hayek (1978). According to Hayek, a clear definition of the laws of property, tort and contract is enough to regulate a set of trial and error exchange relationships, which succeeds in coordinating the plans of an interdependent network of individuals endowed with a multiplicity of competing ends. The process leading to a spontaneous market order takes place in real time with exchanges occurring at out-of-equilibrium prices, it is irreversible, and fatal errors may drive agents out of the market. In contrast, Hayek argues that the notion of competitive general equilibrium based on the *tàtonnement* process, being it no-trade-out-of-equilibrium version of Walras or the provisional contract version of Edgeworth, is "[...] unfortunate, since it presupposes that the facts have already all been discovered and competition, therefore, has ceased" (Hayek, 1978, p. 184). This is not to say that the concept of equilibrium should be definitely abandoned, but simply that the tendency for demands and supplies to adjust so that markets clear can be successfully explained only if we can model it as an emergent feature of economic systems. Since the economy is a complex network of non-linear interactions among adaptive agents, the meaning and the properties of a macroeconomic equilibrium configuration – if it exists – must be qualified, however. First, the presence of non-market interactions imply that decentralized and command solutions do not coincide. Second, even if we can operationally define a social welfare criterion to be somehow maximized, the surface of the objective function is in general very *rugged* and continuously changing. Market forces can drive the system towards a local optimum, and adaptive and imitative individual behaviors may contribute to make it persistent once reached. However, the resulting configuration can be really far from the globally optimal one: market selection due to survival does not imply absolute individual *and* societal optimality.

Summarizing, the complexity approach to economics discards the GE approach to the microfoundation program, as well as its RA shorthand version. Instead of asking to deductively prove the existence of an equilibrium price vector p^* such that $F(p^*)=0$, it aims at explicitly constructing it by means of an algorithm or a rule. From an epistemological perspective, this implies a shift from the realm of classical to that of constructive theorizing (Velupillai, 2002). Clearly, the act of computationally constructing a coordinated state – instead of imposing it via the Walrasian auctioneer – requires a complete description of goal-directed economic agents and of their interaction structure.

As a matter of fact, the complexity view to macroeconomics needs appropriate conceptual and analytical tools. The abandonment of the Walrasian auctioneer implies that market outcomes must be derived from the parallel computations made by a large number of interacting, heterogeneous, adaptive individuals, instead of being deduced as a fixed-point solution to a system of differential equations. The process of removal of externally imposed coordination devices induces a shift from a top-down perspective towards a bottom-up approach. Sub-disciplines of computer science like distributed artificial intelligence and multi-agent systems – computer programs built as loosely coupled networks of software agents that interact to solve problems that are beyond the individual capacities or knowledge of each problem solver – are natural fields to look at. Agent-based computational (ABC) economics – that is the use of computer simulations to grow and study evolving artificial economies composed of many autonomous interacting agents – represents a promising tool for advancements along the research program sketched so far (Judd and Tesfatsion, 2006). [19] The ABC approach allows us to build models with a large number of heterogeneous agents, where the resulting aggregate dynamics is not known *a priori*, and outcomes are not immediately deducible from individual behavior. It is characterized by three main tenets: (*i*) there is a multitude of objects that interact with each other and with the environment; (*ii*) objects are autonomous

[19] The official definition is due to Leigh Tesfatsion (2002, 2006), according to whom: "[...] agent-based computational economics is the computational study of economic processes modelled as dynamic systems of interacting agent".

(hence, they are called *agents*); no central or "top down" control over their behavior is admitted; and (*iii*) the outcome of their interaction is computed numerically.

ABC models have been tested in a sizeable range of applications, where their flexibility has been vastly exploited.[20] In biology, for instance, agents have been modeled as anything from cells to more complex biological entities; in social sciences, agents have been identified either as single individuals and as social groups like families or firms. In all cases a hierarchy can be defined, with higher-order agents being composed by a given number of lower-order agents. The only requirement for this approach is that higher-order agents were perceived from the outside as a unit that "do" something, i.e. they must be able to *act*, to *react* to external stimuli and to *interact* with other agents and the environment surrounding them. The environment, in turn, may include physical entities (infrastructures, geographical locations, etc.) and institutions (markets, regulatory systems, etc.) and, as soon as the conditions outlined above are met, it can be modeled in terms of one or more higher-order agents (e.g. a central bank, the order book of a stock exchange, etc.). If this is not possible, it can be simply thought of as a set of tuneable parameters (say "temperature", or "business confidence"). The *bottom-up* approach to complexity consists therefore in "[…] deducing the macroscopic objects (*macros*) and their phenomenological complex *ad-hoc* laws in terms of a multitude of elementary microscopic objects (*micros*) interacting by simple fundamental laws" (Solomon, 2007), and ABC provides a technique that allows researchers to systematically follow the birth and evolution of these complex macroscopic phenomenology.

Interestingly enough, the *macros* at a specific scale can become the *micros* at the next scale. Depending on the scope of the analysis, in the way down to reconstruct aggregate, top-level dynamics from the bottom up it is generally convenient to stop at some scale. When applied to economics, for example, only a few levels (e.g. a *micro*, a *meso* and a *macro* level) are in general sufficient to provide a thorough understanding of the system.[21]

The need for the ABC approach at any given scale is often linked to the existence of some underlying autocatalytic process at a lower level. Autocatalytic processes are dynamic processes with positive feedbacks, where the growth of some quantity is to some extent self-perpetuating, as in the case when it is proportional to its initial value. The importance of positive feedbacks has been recognized in the literature on increasing returns since the time of Marshall, in particular with respect to the possibility of multiple equilibria (Grüne *et al.*, 2005). However, the traditional analysis is focused on comparative statics, and does not address how an equilibrium out of several might be selected. Looking at the prob-

---

[20] Some examples are Batten (2000), Epstein (2006), Flake (1998), Gilbert and Troitzsch (2005), Miller and Page (2006), Wooldridge (2002).

[21] An interesting strand of literature which allows a micro-meso-macro computational analysis, and that proves to be very close in spirit – and to some extent complementary – to our approach, is the one which applies agent-based techniques to evolutionary Schumpeterian models of endogenous technological change. Inspired by the path-breaking work of Nelson and Winter (1982), recent examples include Dosi *et al.* (2008a, b) and Saviotti and Pyka (2008).

lem from a dynamic stochastic process perspective, selection is explained in terms of one set of small historical events magnified by increasing returns. Moreover, the existence of an autocatalytic process implies that looking at the average, or most probable, behavior of the constituent units is non representative of the dynamics of the system. Hence,

> [...] autocatalyticity insures that the behavior of the entire system is dominated by the elements with the highest auto-catalytic growth rate rather than by the typical or average element. (Solomon, 2007, p. 2)

In presence of autocatalytic processes, even a small amount of individual heterogeneity invalidates any description of the behavior of the system in terms of its "average" element. As a result:

> Much of the real world is controlled as much by the "tails" of the distributions as by means or averages: by the exceptional, not the mean; by the catastrophe, not the steady drip; by the very rich, not the "middle class". We need to free ourselves from "average" thinking. (Anderson, 1997, p. 566)

The fact that autocatalytic dynamics are scale invariant (after a transformation that multiplies all the variables by a common factor) is a key to understanding the emergence of power laws at an aggregate level. The relevance of scale free distributions in economics (e.g. of firm size, wealth, income, etc.) is now extensively recognized (Brock, 1999), and has been the subject of throughout investigations in the econophysics (Mantegna and Stanley, 2000) and macroeconomics (Delli Gatti *et al.*, 2008) literatures.

At this stage, it should appear clear that the methodology of scientific research is the real *litmus paper* of the two competing approaches. Being inspired by logical empiricism, adherents to the NNS argue that the ultimate goal of any positive scientific endeavour is to deploy hypotheses that yield valid and meaningful *predictions* about actual phenomena. Not a single word on predictions at the *meso*-level is spent, let alone about the realism of the starting hypotheses about preferences and beliefs. Even the Occam rule is systematically ignored. For instance, in order to get a downward sloping aggregate demand curve, mainstream economics has to assume indifference curves which are: (*i*) defined only in the positive quadrant of commodity-bundle quantities; (*ii*) negatively sloped; (*iii*) complete; (*iv*) transitive, and (*v*) strictly convex. Moreover, to properly aggregate from microbehavior, the propensity to consume out of income has to be homogeneous for all the agents, and the distribution of endowments must be independent from relative prices (*homothetic* Engel curves).

Compare now the corresponding requirements of an ABC bottom-up model: in order to generate a downward-sloping aggregate demand curve, one has merely to assume the existence of a set of individual reservation prices. That's all! In the bottom-up approach, individual behavior are modeled according to simple behavioral rules; agents are allowed to have *local interaction* and to change the *individual rule* (*through adaptation*) as well as the *interaction nodes*. By aggregating, some *statistical regularity* emerges, which cannot be inferred from individual behavior (*self emerging regularities*): this *emergent behavior* feeds back to the individual level (*downward causation*) thus establishing a macrofoundation of micro (Colander, 1996). As a consequence, each and every proposition may be falsified at *micro*, *meso* and *macro* levels. The distance between this approach and the axiomatic theory of economics, where the optimization procedure is seen as the standard for scientific (i.e. not ad-hoc) modeling looms large.[22]

Reinterpreting Epstein (2006), we can further elucidate the methodology inspiring bottom-up ABC modeling by enumerating a number of key sufficient (although not necessary) conditions to characterize an agent-based model.

Heterogeneity. While in GE models there is a big analytical advantage in reducing the ways in which individuals differ, the computational burden of ABC models is substantially unaffected if different values of the relevant characteristics (e.g. preferences, endowments, location, social contacts, abilities etc.) are specified for different individuals. Usually, this result is attained by choosing a suitable distribution for each characteristic, so that a limited number of parameters (i.e., those governing the corresponding distribution) are added to the model.

Explicit space. This can be seen as a particular substantiation of the previous point: individuals often differ in the physical place where they are located, and/or in the neighbors with whom they are allowed to interact (which define the network structure of the model; see the next point).

Local interaction. ABC models can easily accommodate a wealth of alternative interaction structures. While mainstream models limit themselves to either global (as in Walrasian markets), or very simple local (e.g., 2×2) interaction arrangement, ABC models are particularly suitable in analyzing cases of direct (i.e., not mediated by prices) local (deterministic, as well as stochastic) interactions (Kirman, 1999).[23]

---

[22] According to Beinhocker (2006), complex economies are open-ended, dynamic, non-linear, far from equilibrium systems, while mainstream economics deals with closed, static, linear systems perpetually in equilibrium. Complex systems undertake an evolutionary process of differentiation, selection and amplification, which provides the system itself with novelty and is responsible for its growth in order and complexity.

[23] Actually, the topic of how social relations may affect the allocation of resources has been investigated by some neoclassical economists (e.g., Leibenstein, 1950; Arrow, 1971; Pollack, 1976). However, they went almost completely unheard, until the upsurge in the early 1990s of a brand new body of work aimed at understanding and modelling the social context of economic decisions, usually labelled *new social economics* or *social interaction economics* (Durlauf and Young, 2001). Models of social interactions are generally able to produce several properties, such as *multiple equilibria* (Brock and Durlauf, 2001); *non-ergodicity* and *phase transition* (Durlauf, 1993); *equilibrium stratification* in social and/or spatial dimension (Benabou, 1996; Glaeser *et al.*, 1996); the existence of a *social multiplier* of behaviours (Glaeser *et al.*, 2002). The key idea consists in recognizing that the social relationships in which individual economic agents are embedded can have a large impact on economic decisions. In this literature, the social context impacts on individual economic decisions through several mechanisms. First, social norms, cultural processes and economic institutions may influence motivations, values, and tastes and, ultimately,

Bounded rationality. In models based on a GE solutions, it is generally easier to implement some form of optimal behavior rather than solving models where individuals follow "reasonable" rules of thumb or learn from the experience of others. Interestingly enough, in both cases the opposite is true for ABC models. In particular, bounded rationality enters the picture along two dimensions: either information is private and limited, and agents are endowed with a finite computing capacity. This implies that agents, although typically goal-oriented, use simple heuristics based on local information.[24]

Non-equilibrium dynamics. As explained in Gallegati and Richiardi (2008), from an analytical viewpoint ABC are recursive dynamic systems, in which the state at time t+1 is computed starting from the state at time t. Hence, they allow the investigation of what happens all along the route, not only at the start and at the end of the journey.[25] On the contrary, GE economics *postulates* continuous market clearing, so that every out-of-equilibrium dynamics is discarded from the start, and initial conditions do not matter.

---

make preferences endogenous (Bowles, 1998). Second, even if one admits that individuals are endowed with exogenously given preferences, the pervasiveness of information asymmetries in real-world economies implies that economic agents voluntarily share values, notions of acceptable behaviour and socially based enforcement mechanisms in order to reduce uncertainty and favour coordination (Denzau and North, 1994). Third, the welfare of individuals may depend on some social characteristics like honour, popularity, stigma or status (Cole *et al.*, 1992). Finally, interactions not mediated by enforceable contracts may occur because of pure technological externalities in network industries (Shy, 2001) or indirect effects transmitted through prices (pecuniary externalities) in non-competitive markets (Blanchard and Kyiotaki, 1987), which may lead to coordination failures due to strategic complementarities (Cooper, 1999).

[24] According to the mainstream approach, information is complete and free for all the agents. Note that one of the key assumptions in the Walrasian tradition is that any *strategic behaviour* is ruled out, and the collection of the whole set of the information is left to the market *via* the auctioneer (or a benevolent dictator [Barone, 1908]). In fact, one could read the rational expectation "revolution" as an attempt at decentralising the price setting procedure by defenestrating the auctioneer. Limited information is now taken into account, but the constraints have to affect every agent in the same way (the so-called Lucas' islands hypothesis), while the Greenwald-Stiglitz theorem (Greenwald and Stiglitz, 1986) states that in this case the equilibrium is not even Pareto-constrained. If information is asymmetric or private, agents have to be heterogeneous and direct interaction has to be considered: this simple fact destroys the efficiency property of mainstream model and generates coordination failures. On the contrary, ABM are built upon the hypothesis that agents have limited information and learn through experience and by interacting with other agents.

[25] Brian Arthur offers an effective statement of its relevance for economic theory: "Standard neoclassical economics asks what agents' actions, strategies, or expectations are in equilibrium with (consistent with) the outcome or pattern these behaviours aggregatively create. Agent-based computational economics enables us to ask a wider question: how agents' actions, strategies or expectations might react to – might endogenously change with – the pattern they create. [...] This out-of-equilibrium approach is not a minor adjunct to standard economic theory; it is economics done in a more general way. [...] The static equilibrium approach suffers two characteristic indeterminacies: it cannot easily resolve among multiple equilibria; nor can it easily model individuals' choices of expectations. Both problems are ones of formation (of an equilibrium and of an "ecology" of expectations, respectively), and when analysed in formation – that is, out of equilibrium – these anomalies disappear" (Arthur, 2006, p. 1552).

ABC economics can also be viewed as a practical way to solve the ambiguities surrounding the principle of *methodological individualism*. In its most extreme (and largely erroneous) version, methodological individualism "[...] just means that one starts from the individual in order to describe certain economic relationships" (Schumpeter, 1908, p. 91). This implies that successful explanations of economic social phenomena result from a *separate* analysis of its constituents or, in other terms, that the *explanans* is reduced to the properties, goals and beliefs of individuals. However, it is nowadays clear that any satisfactory explanation of social phenomena – just because of their *social* character – should involve not only a description of the actions of individual agents, but also of the interactive relations between them (Hodgson, 2007). It is precisely here that the GE approach – and thus, its NNS-DSGE rendition – fails (Udhén, 2001). In agent-based models, aggregate outcomes (e.g. the unemployment rate) are computed as the sum of individual behaviors (e.g. individual employment decisions) mediated by social relations. That's why aggregate behavior can often be recognized as distinct from the behavior of the comprising agents, leading to the discovery of emergent properties. In this sense, the whole is more than – and different from – the sum of its parts. It might even be the case that the whole appears to act as if it followed a distinct logic, with its own goals and means, as in the case of a cartel of firms that act in unison in order to influence the market price of a good. A new entity is born; the computational experiment has been successful in "[...] growing artificial societies from the bottom up" (Epstein and Axtell, 1996).

1.4 The Aim and the Contents of this Book

This book arose from our conviction that the NNS-DSGE approach to the analysis of aggregate market outcomes is fundamentally flawed. The practise of overcoming the SMD result by recurring to a fictitious RA leads to insurmountable methodological problems and lies at the root of DSGE models' failure to satisfactorily explain real world features, like exchange rate and banking crises, bubbles and herding in financial markets, swings in the sentiment of consumers and entrepreneurs, asymmetries and persistence in aggregate variables, and so on. At odds with this view, our critique rests on the premise that any modern macroeconomy should be modeled instead as a complex system of heterogeneous interacting individuals, acting adaptively and autonomously according to simple and empirically validated rules of thumb.

We call our proposed approach *Bottom-up Adaptive Macroeconomics* (BAM). The reason why we claim that the contents of this book can be inscribed in the realm of macroeconomics is threefold:

i) We are looking for a framework that helps us to think coherently about the interrelationships among two or more markets. In what follows, in particular, three markets will be considered: the markets for goods, labor and loanable funds. In this respect, real time matters: what happens in one market depends on what has happened, on what is happening, or on what will happen in other markets. This implies that intertemporal coordination issues cannot be ignored.

ii) Eventually, it's all about prices and quantities. However, we are mostly interested in *aggregate* prices and quantities, that is indexes built from the dispersed outcomes of the decentralized transactions of a large population of heterogeneous individuals. Each individual acts purposefully, but she knows anything about the levels of prices and quantities which clear markets in the aggregate.

iii) In the hope of being allowed to purport scientific claims, BAM relies on the assumption that individual purposeful behaviors aggregates into regularities. Macro behavior, however, can depart radically from what the individual units are trying to accomplish. It is in this sense that aggregate outcomes *emerge* from individual actions and interactions.

Agents are autonomous (hence, the qualification *bottom-up*), heterogeneous and bounded rational; imitative learning adds a layer of non-price interaction to individual behavior; and market transactions are completely decentralized. Since the future is uncertain and unforeseeable, historical time becomes central: a decision to produce a given quantity, to change individual prices and wages, or to invest in R&D will affect the future dynamics because of debt commitments and the possibility to incur in fatal mistakes. Price ratios (which depend on autonomous firms' past decisions) and productivity changes are crucial issue in determining future profits. Because of dispersed information, markets are incomplete, and the system fails to mechanically reach a Pareto efficient, even if sub-optimal, general equilibrium position (Greenwald and Stiglitz, 1990).

Chap. 2 is devoted to introduce the key components of our modeling approach. We start from a discussion on the algorithmic nature of the agents populating our artificial world. Individuals are assumed to play the role of simple specialized *processors* which, through decentralized interactions, generate a massively parallel system capable to produce aggregate outcomes through some kind of *emergent computation*. The chapter continues by discussing the agent-based architecture we employ in simulations: the definition of the *classes* of agents, the behavioural rules they obey, how they are allowed to interact, and the methods one can use to analyze the results from simulations.

In Chap. 3 we present a benchmark BAM model. In our approach, the origin of aggregate fluctuations and sustained growth can be traced back to the complex dance of consumption decisions, productivity changes, financial fragility and decentralized out-of-equilibrium trades in an environment characterized by large transaction costs due to strong uncertainty. In the absence of forward markets, the structure of sequential timing implies that firms have to rely on credit to bridge the gap between production decision and realization. Highly leveraged – i.e. financially fragile – firms are exposed to the risk of default. When bankruptcies occur, unemployment increases and the aggregate demand for consumption goods decreases, while non performing loans affect the net worth of the banking system, which reacts reducing the supply of credit. Lower demand and shrinking credit supply increase the risk of bankruptcy economywide. A snowball effect consisting in an avalanche of bankruptcies can follow. Since R&D expenditure is financed out of retained profits, a feedback effect on the long-run growth potential may be easily envisaged along similar lines.

The next topic is the empirical validation – that is, taking the model's results to the data – of our BAM model. Chap. 4 is devoted to it. First, we present evidence on the macroeconomic time series emerging from simulations, as well as on the distributional dynamics of industrial and financial variables. Second, Italian data are applied to a validation exercise performed by means of microsimulation techniques. Our results are in general encouraging, in some cases even striking.

Chap. 5 concludes the book by summarizing the main arguments treated in previous chapters, and advancing some lines of future research. In particular, we argue for the need of a deep rethinking of actual macroeconomic theory, one rooted in the science of complexity.

Chapter 2
The Making of the *BAM* Model

> Into the determination of … prices and wages there will enter the effects of particular information possessed by every one of the participants in the market process – a sum of facts which in their totality cannot be known to the scientific observer, or to any other single brain. It is indeed the source of the superiority of the market order … that in the resulting allocation of resources more of the knowledge of particular facts will be utilized which exists only dispersed among uncounted persons, than any one person can possess. But because we … can thus never know all the determinants of such an order, and in consequence also cannot know at which particular structure of prices and wages demand would everywhere equal supply, we also cannot measure the deviations from that order.
>
> FRIEDRICH A. VON HAYEK
> *The Pretence of Knowledge*, p. 12

2.1 A Theory of the *Economic Agent*

The illuminating prose of Friedrich von Hayek illustrates some of the main issues that are at the core of the bottom-up approach to macroeconomics we offer in this book. The inhabitants of the realistic economies we aim to model form expectations and take actions building on the asymmetric and incomplete information they acquire by exploring limited portions of space and time, while their dispersed market transactions generate aggregate outcomes whose welfare properties are unknowable in principle, at least if one pretends to measure them against some hypothetical Walrasian general equilibrium. The quotation has also a second value added in that it helps us to stress once again that this vision, though considered as heretical by the mainstream, does not represent anything particularly new from a theoretical viewpoint. On the contrary, it is part and parcel of a well-honored but guiltily disregarded tradition in the history of economic thought, one that considers the economic agent as a proper human being instead of a computer-like automaton. We argue that it is time not only to bring this tradition back to life, but also to revamp it by means of new insights from other behavioral sciences, like cognitive psychology and social biology.

In particular, the theoretical description of the economic agent we endorse is rooted in the so-called *program-based behavior* paradigm (Mayr, 1988; Vanberg, 2002; 2004), according to which goal-seeking, purposeful activities are guided by encoded algorithmic programs or instructions, telling agents what to do (or not to do) when facing certain contingencies. These rules for action may sometimes be sophisticated enough to integrate multiple sources of information into the building of mental models, that is internal representations that the agent creates to interpret and manipulate his own problem space, or to form aspirations and commitments into the future, or finally to sign forward contracts or other arrangements with terminal dates in the future (Denzau and North, 1994). Knowledge feeding the cognitive and deliberative courses of action is acquired through adaptive, evolutionary learning processes in a truly uncertain and ever-changing environment. Action-guiding programs and repertoires of rules are then selected by means of reinforcement and recombination procedures which are activated as the agent encounters new situations (Holland, 1988; 1996). Internal models are retained inasmuch as they continue to guarantee a satisfactory understanding of the outer world and of the implications of chosen actions, but they are discarded as they become patently obsolete, just to be replaced by new ones.

More generally, however, evolutionary argumentations suggest that the real-time rules for action human beings adopt are more often than not consistent – and compelled to be in line – with much more rapid decision making than the ones based on evolving mental models. It appears that not always human adaptation is guided by internal models of the world which the brain takes as defining the constraints for logic calculations aimed at solving analytical problems. In some situations, it would simply take too much time and it would employ too many neural resources. Rather, actions must respond to very simple rules aimed at coping promptly and effectively with the environment. This is precisely the point raised by a body of active research at the intersection of artificial intelligence, robotics, cognitive sciences and connectionist philosophy, of which M. Minsky (1986), Churchland and Sejnowski (1992) and Clark (1997) represent outstanding examples. Simply stated, their thesis is that it is critically misleading to model the human mind as a kind of logical reasoning device apt to symbolic manipulation, joined to a memory bank of facts. The process of natural selection – with its call for speedy responses in real-world situations, where mere survival is at stake – has forced human intelligence to operate in a way completely different from that of a central computer program solving a maximization problem does.

At odds with the theoretical position which portrays the mind as a logical symbol-processing machine, in fact, human intelligence emerges from the use of very simple rules and strategies to cope quickly and effectively with environmental hazards – such as the need for food, the presence of predators, and the like – and strong uncertainties on the behavior of other members of the social group. Accordingly, human intelligence is ultimately a means for controlling the body's set of behaviors to help it survive in the particular environment it happens to live in or, in other terms, it provides a form of "embodied, environmentally embedded cognition" (Clark, 1997). The bulk of the connectionist approach relies on a computational architecture consisting of a mass of interacting "neurons" – simple autonomous processing units receiving inputs from neighboring units and passing on output to other neighbors – usually organized in layers. Activity is then propagated through the network by weighted connections between units, so that the system as a whole allows knowledge in terms of distributed encoding. This does not amount to downplay the role of large hierarchical structures operating specialized processing duties (visual cortex, hippocampus, etc.), but simply to recognize that the main job is eventually done by single units:

> The anatomy of the frontal cortex and other areas beyond the primary sensory areas suggests an information organization more like the Athenian democracy than a Ford assembly line. Hierarchies typically have an apex, and following the analogy, one might expect to find a brain region where all sensory information converges and from which motor commands emerge. It is a striking fact that this is false of the brain. Although there are convergent pathways, the convergence is partial and occurs in many places many times over, and motor control appears to be distributed rather than vested in a central command center. (Curchland and Sejnowski, 1992, pp. 24–25)

The brain is thus a massively parallel system, in which control and information processing are distributed among autonomous but interacting units, who appear to an external observer as coordinating themselves to jointly solve some identifiable problem, through some kind of emergent computation. Connectionist scientists argue that this is the real essence of intelligence, and this position has profound implications for the concept of rationality as it is usually applied in economics.

According to received tradition of the discipline, in fact, the behavioral core of economics resides in the so-called rational choice theory (Becker, 1976). This is based on two ingredients. First, it is assumed that human action is rational if the entire system of beliefs and preferences is internally consistent on the one hand, and if it is consistent with actual choices on the other one. Second, rational agents should also hold true beliefs about the outer world. Since its formal definition, the faith of economists on this assumption has proved to be complete. Indeed, full or substantial rationality – and its substantiation made of dynamic programming methods to calculate optima – has rapidly became a benchmark against which failures or deficiencies – for instance, in terms of computational capabilities – can be measured and assessed. Since the presumption of fully rational human behavior is patently false, bounded rationality (Simon, 2000) is in one way or another accepted and justified for the sake of realism, but in the backstage it continues to remain implicitly assumed that if cognitive constraints could be somehow successfully relaxed, fully rationality could in principle re-enter the scene.

Notice the difference with the connectionist approach. Now, economic intelligence and rationality do not coincide with the ability to solve huge analytical problems by means of a centralized (a *homunculus* located somewhere in the brain) computer-type device manipulating large data structures. By contrast, they entail the joined efforts of a decentralized network of autonomous and interacting neurons giving rise to a kind of emergent distributed computation, which endows the individual with simple tricks and strategies mapping situations into actions speedily, in a way that is well adapted to his environment, both natural and social.

Along these lines it can be argued that the standard *as if* claim used by mainstream economists to defend the rationality principle is just an expression of faith with faulty epistemological foundations. Milton Friedman, for instance, repeatedly used examples such as driving a car to claim that humans are ultimately capable of solving complicated optimization problems like the one specified in neoclassical economics. Optimization, however, is a technique that is appropriate only when there is a known set of future outcomes and known probabilities associated with each occurrence. The problem of driving a car – and, more interestingly for us, of performing many other activities like consuming, producing and trading in competitive markets – is that of generating fast, smooth and environmentally appropriate actions precisely when the environment is strongly uncertain. A more plausible neuroscientific model is one that replaces a central planning processing string of manipulable symbols with a complex network of encoding schemes and basic operations of pattern recognition and pattern transformation. Higher-level mental representations are used almost unconsciously when needed, as when one swerves routinely to the right to avoid a frontal collision with a car supervening in the opposite direction along a very narrow road, simply because it is implicitly and unconsciously assumed that the other driver is used to drive on the right and he will swerve rightward as well.[26]

From this viewpoint, a decentralized competitive economy – that is, one which gets rid of any central planner – is just a higher-order massively parallel system composed of many autonomous individual economic processors, namely intelligent human beings, who use (simple) rules to set prices, make production and consumption decisions, search, communicate and exchange in order to improve their welfare. The decentralization characterizing real competitive markets is in fact the key: it works as a powerful distributed algorithm to collectively solve computationally complex allocative problems which are far beyond the cognitive capabilities – and even the awareness – of individual agents (Rust, 1998). This is another way to maintain that the economy is a complex adaptive system (Leijonhufvud, 2006). While it has not been formally proven yet that this type of distributed computational device is able to reach efficiency under general conditions, previous research has shown clearly that the coordination performance of a multi-market system depends on the – market (e.g. double auction, limit orders, etc.) and non-market (e.g. customs, norms, etc.) – institutions providing structure to human actions and interactions (Gode and Sunder, 1993). Agent-based modeling is a natural candidate for further explorations along this dimension.

In viewing a macroeconomy as a complex adaptive system a last issue deserves to be emphasized, that is the autonomy of agents. As discussed at length in Tesfatsion

[26] The authors of this book have all learnt to drive a car in a continental European country. The outcome would be dramatically different if at least one of the two drivers in our example would come from the UK.

(2006), in market-clearing models the prices and quantities chosen by an individual agent cannot be specified independently of the choices actually made by the others, or the rational expectation thereof, but they are bounded to be consistent with an equilibrium state that someone outside the model (the WA) has calculated without the use of scarce resources. In other terms, in market-clearing models the behavior of agents is bound to be interconnected in correspondence of the equilibrium configuration, it doesn't matter how deep on microeconomic foundations one is willing to dig. This amounts to assuming away any possibility to study real coordination problems. The agents living in the artificial world we will discuss in the next chapter, on the contrary, are endowed with behavioral rules telling them what to do in any given situation, independently of what everyone else in the economy is doing. Aggregate coordination, if it happens to occur, should be an emergent property of the system and not a superimposition of the modeler.

2.2 Setting the Stage

In order to force the complexity of the real world into manageable theoretical frameworks, scientists are used to adopt the reasonable epistemological device of abstracting from some of the characteristics of the particular elements they observe and group them into *classes*. The more audacious the abstraction is, the wider the classes one ends up with.

In their attempts to relate the behavior of a myriad of individual decision-makers to the aggregate quantitative data they can effectively collect and organize, economists have been second to none as regards this type of generalization. Classical thinkers like Adam Smith, David Ricardo and Karl Marx saw the economy as an articulation of *social classes* – workers, capitalists and *rentiers* – in a typical structuralist approach: the individual behavior of the member of a class is of any importance only insofar it substantiates the behavior of the class itself as a whole. The marginalist revolution led by Stanley Jevons and Irving Fisher subverted this approach by modeling human beings as rational choosers. The field of application of rational choice theory now simply depends on the nature of endowments, so that the chooser is a worker if she is endowed with labor-power, and she becomes an entrepreneur if she is endowed with physical and organizational capital. What usually remains in modern macroeconomic models after this pooling process is just one class of homogeneous households (workers/consumers) and one class of homogeneous firms.[27] The representative yeoman assumption pushes this simplifying procedure to its extremes, considering essentially a macroeconomic system

[27] This is of course the simplest conceivable setting in the simplest case of a closed economy without public sector. Also in this setting, there are richer models which consider also other classes of agents, such as banks, investors on financial markets, etc. In any case, a relatively small (very small) number of classes are considered. Usually, the number and type of classes is a prior of the modeler.

populated by one agent, who consumes what she produces by employing the labor and the capital services she optimally offers to herself.

In what follows we allow for partial or complete specialization in economic activities (consumption, production, labor supply and demand, trading) inside a large economic system by borrowing concepts and expressions from object-oriented programming (Jennings *et al.*, 1998; Weisfeld, 2004).[28] In formal terms, an *object* is an algorithmic description (in our case, lines of software code inside a larger computer program) of a purposive entity with some identifiable and specialized *features*. Each object contains a list of *attributes* and a set of *methods* acting on these attributes. An object can control the mode of external access to its attributes and methods, by declaring them public (accessible to all), private (inaccessible to all) or protected (accessible only to some other objects). A *class* is then defined as a template or blueprint for the instantiation of objects sharing those common but peculiar features. As a result, we can state the following:

Assumption 1. The fundamental starting point of our analysis is the simple methodological assumption according to which any economic system (*synthetic world*) consists of *classes*. Each class consists of a very large number N of agents (*objects*) who are heterogeneous according to a certain number (n) of different criteria (*attributes*).

For example, objects that belong to the class of *firms* (units whose role is that of using productive inputs to produce final goods, and choosing quantities and prices) will be characterized by heterogeneity of size, financial condition and technology; members of the class of *households* (units which offer labor, consume goods, save precautionally) will be characterized by different employment status, labor income and savings; objects belonging to the class of *banks* (units which provide funds) will be characterized by different internal financial conditions. Therefore, in a sense, we start by classifying agents in general *types*, but at odds with standard macroeconomics we allow for substantial heterogeneity of individual characteristics.

This is not exactly a novel feature of macroeconomic models. A very simple example of a framework suitable for macro-analysis which incorporates heterogeneity is the Overlapping Generations (OLG) framework where agents differ because of their age, and are therefore classified in two types (young and old). This is an example of the simplest conceivable setting to deal with heterogeneity: there is only *one* criterion to classify agents ($n=1$), and there are only *two* types ($N=2$).[29]

Once we depart from this simplest setting, we can easily get lost in the wilderness of heterogeneity, as both the criteria and the types can asymptotically tend to infinity. The most complicated conceivable setting is in fact characterized by $n \rightarrow \infty$, $N \rightarrow \infty$. Clearly, pushing heterogeneity of objects and attributes to these limits –

[28] See McFazdean and Tesfatsion (1999) for an introduction to object-oriented programming into economics, and an application to the endogenous formation of trading networks.

[29] Of course there can be many agents in any generation, but they are ultimately uniform. Each young (old) is a clone of any other young (old). Therefore, despite the appearance of a very large number of agent, the model boils down to only two of them.

i.e. allowing for a continuum of different agents identified according to an extremely large number of classifying criteria – is neither useful nor particularly realistic. The end result of this extreme strategy would be a model with the same relevance and usefulness of a geographic chart characterized by the scale 1:1, as Joan Robinson once said mocking models whose degree of complexity is unmanageable.

Once the issue of finiteness is taken into account, however, a new problem emerges. In fact, there is no compelling reason to propose and follow a particular rule in picking up finite values of n and N inside the infinite set of integers. We have a preference, however, for models with a relatively *small* n – but $n >> 1$ – and a relatively *large* N. In other words, we prefer models with many types of agents but a relatively small set of criteria to classify agents by type. This choice is essentially dictated by a preference for realism (large N) in a relatively simple and manageable setting (small n) and leads us to build models – such as the following one and the one discussed in our previous book (EM) – which can be characterized as *multi-agent models*.

How small should n be? This is actually a matter of convenience. In other terms, the choice is dictated by the problem at hand. In our models, for instance, we cannot abstract from the heterogeneity of financially-oriented agents – essentially, firms and banks – and this choice is crucial for the analysis of short run fluctuations. When long run growth is the core of the analysis, in turn, heterogeneity in technology adoption becomes crucial.

How large should N be? The largest possible, given the constraints due to computational power. Sometimes, however, there is no need to resort to a very fine partition of a particular class of agents. In some cases, a binary choice may be enough, for instance by recurring to the presence or absence of some qualitative features (e.g., employed/unemployed). Alternatively, a binary partition can be imposed by resorting to a threshold value which splits a quantitative domain into two subsets. In the case of financial conditions, for example, in principle there may be an infinity of different types (due, for instance to their leverage). We can nonetheless partition the population of agents in two groups – rich and poor – choosing a threshold level of leverage. The choice of the threshold is almost always characterized by some degree of arbitrariness.

2.3 Rules of Behavior

Once classes and agents (objects defined by attributes) have being created, specific statements must be made as regards how the agents themselves are allowed to process information, and to act consequently. Our choice is summarized in the following:

Assumption 2. Agents are characterized by simple *behavioral rules* (methods acting on attributes), that is stylized (algorithmic) patterns of economic behavior. Each agent may follow different – say, ν – rules due to different circumstances, i.e. different time periods, geographical areas, markets, and so on.

In principle, these rules may or may not be the outcome of an optimizing process. Optimization yields the smallest possible set of rules, because once one fully specifies the pre-requisites of any optimization procedure – objective functions, constraints, and information sets – under conditions of regularity there is only one behavior the agent can rationally follow, i.e. the optimal one. In symbols, this sort of situational determinism due to optimization yields $\nu = 1$.

By definition, optimization requires both top-down cognitive capabilities for symbolic programming and a stable environment. As discussed above, in this book we argue in favor of a parallel distributed model of both the human brain and of a society composed of a multitude of brains, each one of them employing "fast and frugal" heuristics whenever involved in various kinds of collective and environment-exploiting problem solving activities. Once we choose to get rid of optimization, however, we can easily get lost in the wilderness of ad-hoc behavioral rules, as there is not in principle any constraint on the types of behavioral rules one can adopt. In symbols, $\nu \to \infty$. Pushing heterogeneity to this limit, that is a continuum of different behavioral rules, makes the model – especially a multi-agent model – easily unmanageable.

There is no compelling reason to propose and follow a given number of rules in picking up ν into the infinite set of integers. We have a preference for models with a relatively *small* ν – sometimes even $\nu = 1$ – even if we adopt a behavioral perspective. In other words, we prefer models with many types of agents but a relatively small set of behaviors for each class of agents. This choice is essentially dictated by a fondness for realism and manageability. Under the paradigm of embodied, environmentally embedded cognition discussed above, it is very unlikely that agents are so sophisticated to adopt a large number of different behavioral rules. It is much more plausible to assume a relatively small ν.

The choice of the behavioral rule may be done on the basis of the empirical literature – a sort of "calibration" of the model based on experimental data on actual microeconomic behavior – or, if possible, by simply asking people how they behave in their ordinary business life, as in survey studies. When the modeler has no clue coming from the empirical literature, the obvious choice is to run the model with different competing behavioral rules and compare them in terms of how good they are in generating results that fit the available empirical evidence. The rule that comes first in its ability to reproduce stylized facts is the one to be adopted.

What is in our view a behavioral rule, then? It is first and foremost a relationship between an *action*, i.e. a specific level of a *control or decision variable* and the levels of the *state variables* that characterize the agent. Suppose, for simplicity, that there are κ control variables and σ state variables for each agent. Let $\underline{C}_{it}$ be the (κ, 1) vector[30] of control variables available to agent i in period t and $\underline{S}_{it}$ the (σ, 1) vector of state variables characterizing the agent in the same period. Since the current action is likely to affect the state in the same period, logically,

[30] In what follows, underscores denote vectors.

the present action is affected by the state of the agent in the past. Hence the simplest conceivable formulation for a behavioral rule is the following:

$$\underline{C}_{it} = C_i(\underline{S}_{it-1}) . \tag{2.1}$$

The present action will contribute to the current state of the agent and therefore indirectly to the future action the agent is going to take. Hence:

$$\underline{S}_{it} = F_i(\underline{S}_{it-1}, \underline{C}_{it}) = F_i\left(\underline{S}_{it-1}, C_i\left(\underline{S}_{it-1}\right)\right) . \tag{2.2}$$

Equation (2.2) represents the law of motion of the state variables which govern the evolution over time of the features characterizing the individual agent. It is a σ-dimensional generally non-linear dynamical system, which maps the overall state of agent i in t–1, as captured by $\underline{S}_{it-1}$, in the state of the agent in t, $\underline{S}_{it}$. Of course, there are N of these dynamical laws, one for each agent. The evolution over time of the macroeconomy, therefore, is described by a system of (Nxσ) difference equations.

Notice that, by construction, such a (Nxσ) system is so far composed of unrelated equations, since the behavior of each individual is considered as secluded from the rest of the world. Each agent's state is in fact evolving over time only on the basis of her own states in the past, and it does not depend on the evolution of the states of the other agents in the economy. In other words, each agent evolves – and therefore can be analyzed – in isolation. This is patently and unnecessarily unrealistic. We have to move a step further in the direction of modeling economic behavior in a fully integrated macroeconomic system by taking into account the fundamental role of interaction.

2.4 Interaction

Everyday experience suggests that human beings bargain and trade with each other, join up together to form organizations for pursuing common aims, communicate with each other, and learn from each other. In other terms, individual agents participate to and contribute to that complex network called *society*, in which they do interact in a number of ways.

In order to introduce into our framework the issue of *social interaction* in the simplest way, we make use of the following:

Assumption 3. The actions of the individual $\underline{C}_{it}$ in t are affected by the *collective* actions of other agents in the past, captured here by the vector of some summary statistics (say, the averages) of cross-sectional control variables, $\underline{E}_{t-1}$.

For the sake of simplicity, we will assume that individual control variables are not affected by other agents' *individual* actions in a *strategic* setting. In other words, on the one hand the ith agent is indeed affected by the population at large consisting of the N–1 remaining agents – with N large enough to make the contribution of i to the aggregate "negligible" – and she may be also aware of this influence but she is not intentionally "playing" a game against each of the other agents. On the other hand agent i is indeed contributing – as one of the N–1 remaining agents – to shape the state of the jth agent but only as one minuscule component of an aggregate which is meant to describe the collective behavior of the population at large.

Assumption 3 leads to the following reformulation of (2.1):

$$\underline{C}_{it} = C_i(\underline{S}_{it-1}, \underline{E}_{t-1}). \tag{2.3}$$

Therefore, in order to account for (2.3), equation (2.2) must be "augmented" as follows:

$$S_{it} = F_i(\underline{S}_{it-1}, \underline{C}_{it}) = F_i\left(\underline{S}_{it-1}, C_i(\underline{S}_{it-1}, \underline{E}_{t-1})\right). \tag{2.4}$$

The presence of the vector $\underline{E}_{t-1}$ in the expression above captures the idea that the state of the individual agent is affected by an average of all the actions taken by all other agents, a type of interaction that physicists call of the *mean-field* type.

Equation (2.4) represents the law of motion of the state variables which governs the evolution over time of the "features" characterizing each individual agent. Again, it is a σ-dimensional generally non-linear dynamical system; of course, there are N of these dynamical systems, one for each agent. Notice that, by construction, now the system (2.4) is *not* strictly individual. Each agent's state is evolving over time not only on the basis of her own past states, but also on the basis of the average state of the economy represented by $\underline{E}_{t-1}$. All in all, the dynamical system is composed of a system of (Nxσ) *coupled* difference equations, where the coupling is due to the mean-field interaction.

In fact, real agents interact with each other in many alternative ways, that can be classified according to several, overlapping criteria. As it will appear patent in a while, some types of interaction have been already considered in standard macroeconomics. However, the one and only way for dealing with them has been to consider them as externalities and realize that they cause a wedge between individual and social welfare.

The ***first criterion*** is based on the type of impact the action of an agent has on the other agents. According to the first criterion, in fact, interaction can be

- ***Direct***: when the action of an agent (or of a set of agents) directly affects the internal state of the agents with whom she is connected.
- ***Indirect***: when the action of an agent affects the state of the other agents only indirectly.

Some descriptive examples will help us to illustrate the point. A first, self-explaining instance of direct interaction is the case of a firm which hires (create a contractual linkage) or fires (severe a contractual linkage) a worker. A less straightforward example is the case of a household which tries to *keep up with the Joneses*, i.e. it imitates the consumption pattern of its neighbors. In this case, the average consumption of the neighborhood directly affects the consumption of the agent.

As regards indirect interaction, a classic example is the following. Suppose that, absent market power, a large number of relatively small, anonymous transactions determines an *equilibrium* price on a specific market. Suppose moreover that, due to the collapse of consumers' confidence, all of a sudden the market price goes down because of an unexpected exogenous contraction of market demand. In the economists' jargon, this is the first step (the *impact*) of an *adjustment process* consisting in a downward trajectory of the market price in the presence of excess supply of the good. The single agent who is currently looking for a bargain on that market is *indirectly* affected through the decrease of the market price by the aggregate consumption pattern (determined by the crisis of consumers confidence) of the rest of the economy. Being now the good cheaper because of the adjustment process, the agent will be eager to purchase a larger amount. This is true also for all other agents, of course. A widespread tendency to increase expenditure will show up in the market, which can be characterized as the *second round* effect of the shock. The second round effect plays a *stabilizing* role, due essentially to a negative feedback, attenuating the downward dynamic pattern of the market price until a new equilibrium price is reached. It is not difficult to recognize here the textbook *story* usually attached to the adjustment process on a specific market.

How does market power change the picture? Suppose that some agents, being endowed with a certain degree of market power, are actually posting prices on the same market we have considered above. In this case, a change of the equilibrium market price may be induced by a change of behavior of these pivotal agents. In this scenario, the single agent who is currently looking for a bargain is *indirectly* affected through the decrease of the market price induced by the behavior of these big players or market-makers. The essence of the first and second round effects discussed previously remains unaltered.

Another important example of indirect interaction can be appreciated by arguing along the following lines (Stiglitz and Greenwald, 2003; Delli Gatti *et al.* 2005). Suppose that the equilibrium interest rate on loans is determined by a large number of credit contracts in a market for bank loans. Suppose moreover that, due for instance to a financial crisis, a non negligible number of borrowers goes bankrupt. A loss due to non-performing loans shows up in the banks' balance sheet. Banks react to this deterioration of their financial conditions by restraining the quantity of new loans and/or making credit conditions harder for the borrowers. This leads to a sudden increase of the market interest rate. The single (surviving) agent who is currently looking for a loan on that market is *indirectly* affected through the increase of the interest rate by the aggregate solvency (determined by the crisis and the associated bankruptcies) of the borrowers. Credit being now more expensive because of the adjustment process of the market price of credit, i.e. the interest rate, the agent will be more cautious in getting into debt. This is true also of the other agents, of course. A tendency to reduce indebtedness will spread among borrowers. This second round effect plays a *stabilizing* role, attenuating the upward dynamic pattern of the interest rate.

In this example, however, this is not the end of the story. In a setting characterized by heterogeneous financial conditions, the increase of the interest rate is likely to be lethal to those firms which were already on the verge of bankruptcy because of an extremely low level of net worth. In other words, these firms will be pushed out of the market. The balance sheets of the lenders will be negatively affected by this new wave of bankruptcies, so that they will react by pushing even further up the interest rate. This too is a second round effect, but it plays a de-*stabilizing* role, exacerbating the upward dynamic pattern of the interest rate. In conclusion, there are two types of second-round effects at work here: the first one is essentially a negative feedback effect with a stabilizing role, while the second one is a positive feedback effect with a destabilizing role. With a slight abuse of terminology, this second round effect can be defined as a *financial accelerator*.

Notice that in last two examples interaction occurs through an assumed *market equilibrium*. In the narrative above we have skipped the thorny issues of existence, stability and attainability of equilibrium on purpose: from the story we told, in fact, it is not clear if out-of-equilibrium transactions were allowed or not. As already discussed, a consistent neoclassical picture is not complete if one ignores the role of the WA, who keeps track of the changes in excess supply over time but prevents transactions out of equilibrium (i.e. at a "false price") until a new equilibrium is reached. Transactions at false prices in fact would change agents' endowment during the transition to equilibrium and therefore distort the process of price formation. In a truly decentralized system there is no certainty about equilibrium attainment, even if transactions can sometimes self-organize into situations which can be assimilated to attainable equilibria by autonomous and heterogeneous agents employing plausible simple rules.

According to the ***second criterion***, which focuses on the spatial range of the relationships, interactions can be:

- ***Local***: when the action of an agent (or of a set of agents) affects the state of only a *few* other agents grouped in a neighborhood.
- ***Global***: when each agent can in principle interact with any other agent.

Local interaction is customarily assumed and justified on the basis of transaction and informational costs, which prevent agents from exploring the whole market landscape in finite time, and force them to search only limited and fixed portions of it. Whenever there is no definite structure determining who interacts with whom, on the contrary, matching between pairs of agents can be supposed to occur randomly. Provided each individual may potentially come into contact with every other member of the population, the interaction structure which emerges as agents search through random sampling for new deals and new pieces of information can be defined as global.

According to the ***third criterion***, we can distinguish between:

- ***Market interactions***: when interactions are mediated by market prices.
- ***Non-market interactions***: when they are not mediated by prices.

A simple example will help to grasp the point. Suppose a consumer wants to ascertain market conditions (posted price and available quantity) for a certain good. She incurs at least the cost of moving from one spot/seller to another to get the information she needs. Therefore the process of search for the best bargain and matching is inherently characterized by transaction costs. In order to economize on such costs, the consumer will visit only a few of the firms which produce the good in question. In this setting each agent has to choose her peer, or reference, group *P*. The reference group is a subset of agents (within the population) whom the agent is to interact with in a specific situation. For example, the consumer choosing a group of shopkeepers whom to buy from is actually choosing her peer group on the consumption good market. Learning and information sharing will occur, period after period, inside the group. This is an instance of direct non-market interaction. Subsequently, inside the peer group agents belonging to the opposite sides of the market engage in a proper market interaction. The most obvious example of this market interaction is the implementation of a transaction.

The same kind of one-to-many interactions among agents belonging to different classes characterizes many markets – for instance, the credit and the labor markets – where customer relations, relationship-credit arrangements and long-term employer-employee attachments are frequently observed.

According to the ***fourth criterion***, interactions can affect:

- ***Preferences***: when the preference ordering over the choice set of one agent depends directly on the actions chosen by other agents.
- ***Constraints***: when changes in one agent's action modifies the feasible set of another agent, affecting indirectly the set of choices available to the latter.
- ***Expectation formation***: when an agent forms expectations observing other agents' behavior or mimicking other agents' expectations.

Interactions concerning preferences have been analyzed in economics at least since the pioneering work of Thorstein Veblen (1899) on *conspicuous consumption*. Two different mechanisms have been highlighted in the sizeable literature on interacting preferences that followed such a masterpiece: people are influenced directly in their choices by what others are doing or are planning to do either because of a desire to emulate, to acquire *status*, and to *keep up with the Joneses*; or because they fear to be punished or ostracized if their behavior does not conform with the most common choices within a reference group.

Constraints also are affected – albeit indirectly – by the interaction of the type we have considered in the examples above. When changes in the aggregate behavior of the rest of the economy act upon the equilibrating variable and the latter – such as the market price – is a datum for the decision making process of the single agent (in the absence of market power), the choice set of the agent end up being affected indirectly by the behavior of the rest of economy.

Let us pause briefly on expectation formation. In a setting characterized by uncertainty agents have to form expectations to complete the decision making process, by attributing in period t a value to variable x will assume at time $t+1$ in a non-deterministic environment. In the standard macroeconomic framework – characterized by individual rationality and *adequate* computational capability – each agent acts "as an econometrician" running rolling regressions on a dataset which is continuously updated by incoming data from the economy.[31] Apparently there is no interaction with other agents, but this conclusion is wrong. It is true that each agent is running regressions independently from the others, but the data that are flowing period after period on the actual behavior of the variable x are indeed influenced by the expectations of every agent. And these data feed back on future expectations, since each agent uses them to run regressions. There are indeed two types of feedback at work here: one from expectations to data, and one from data to expectations.

The fixed point of this process, under appropriate circumstances, identifies the so-called Rational Expectations (RE) equilibrium, hence the name *rational learning* attached to this approach. The rolling regressions procedure, in this case, allows the agents to discover the true model of the economy (at least in its reduced form). The "representative agent" will therefore hold rational expectations so that on average forecast errors are equal to zero.

Of course this process of running rolling regressions does not always yield the RE equilibrium. The sequential feedbacks of expectations on the actual variable and of the latter on expectations, however, are an important part of any story concerning expectations' formation. But the interaction is only *indirect* through the first feedback. Expectation formation on the part of each and every agent feeds back on the market value of the variable, which is a datum that each and every agent is using to run regressions.

There can be direct interaction in expectations' formation, however, when, due to incomplete or asymmetric information an agent is actually "borrowing" the expectation of her neighbor or of the average of her neighboring agents. This is the case of herding. Here the agent is characterized as lacking rationality or computational capability so that she economizes on the cost of acquiring additional information or computational power by mimicking the expectations' formation of her peers. In this case, expectations can well be different and heterogeneity can be persistent.

Admittedly, in microeconomics interactions have always played a crucial role. Market interaction is at the root of the Walrasian approach to general equilibrium, since the adjustment of the price to changes in demand or supply is governed by the impersonal (indirect) interaction occurring between agents of the two sides of the market (supply and demand) mediated by the price level. Non-market interactions – that is those not regulated by the price mechanism – have been characterized as externalities and are at the root of the standard theory of market failures.

We cannot say the same for macroeconomics: in this case "interaction" is far too ambiguous a word. The myriad of interactions occurring in the real world *within* a class of agents (for instance among firms) are considered negligible and therefore simply ignored. Interactions *between classes* (for instance between firms and households) are essentially of the indirect/market type, i.e. they generally surface in macroeconomics as an adjustment mechanism of an equilibrating variable in a specific market. For instance, excess aggregate demand for consumption goods in a macroeconomic model of the Keynesian type yields a generalized in-

[31] For a complete analysis of these issues, see Evans and Honkapoija (2004).

voluntary reduction of inventories and provides an incentive for producers to increase the scale of production in the market for consumption goods. Each class is represented by the average agent, so that these interactions are reduced to *mean-field* interaction.

In statistical physics, a mean-field representation of interaction is a device to capture the essence of the myriad of micro interactions among particles by means of an approximation which replaces them with the interaction of a particle with the average of the remaining particles. In a nutshell, in a mean-field representation of social interaction, the intricate pattern of the myriad of interactions of one agent's action – say agent A – with any other agent – B, C, D … – are replaced by the interaction of the same agent with the *average* of the actions taken by the agents. This reduces the dimensionality of the interaction from a multi-agent problem to a one-agent problem. Interactions among agents are replaced by interactions among the *means* of the choice variables of *classes* of agents.[32]

All in all, the only kind of interaction contemplated by macroeconomics is definitely a mean-field one, and therefore mainstream macroeconomic theories are ultimately theories of means. Of course, one may wonder whether the mean is representative of the class. An obvious answer is that the mean is representative, properly speaking, only when one agent populates each class, i.e. when the higher moments of the distribution of agents' characteristics goes asymptotically to zero! But if this is not the case, we need to search for some alternative representations ensuring meaningfulness to the means.

In other words, once the rules of actions of individual units have been characterized analytically, the key theoretical problem of *aggregation* shows up: having defined the *micro-equations* representing the choices of individual economic units, what can be said about *macro-equations*? Do these latter have the same functional form of the former (*exact aggregation*)? If not, how can we derive macro-equations, and in what relationship do they stand with micro-equations?

It is well known that exact aggregation requires a set of extremely implausible restrictions, like linearity and homogeneity of micro relationships or mean-scaled distributions of relative variables (Gorman, 1954; Jorgenson *et al.*, 1982; Lewbel, 1989). There have been attempts at escaping from these limitations by adopting simplifying shortcuts or stochastic aggregation methods (Kalejan, 1980; Stoker, 1984). Some methods are also available to deal with cross-sectional heterogeneity and interactions (at least if they remain constrained to the mean-field type) at the same time (Aoki, 2001; Palestrini *et al.*, 2006). It must be recognized, however, that the very issue of aggregation has been so far systematically ignored in the macroeconomics literature, a point which sheds an ominous light on its scientific credentials.

---

[32] Notice that on this particular modeling choice the Keynesian and Neoclassical frames of thought are indistinguishable. The differences are the laws supposed to underlie the behavior of the means: in fact, according to Keynesians it is sufficient to study a "working" relationship between, for example, aggregate consumption and aggregate income; while, according to the Neoclassical reductionist approach, the mean outcomes have to be derived as if they were the optimal responses by a representative consumer or firm.

The reliance on mean outcomes by mainstream macroeconomics is based in fact on the maintained belief that idiosyncratic shocks cancel out in the aggregate. But this condition holds true only once a particular property, extensively used in physics and known as *self-averaging* (Sornette, 2000), is established.

Formally, a size-dependent (random) variable x, characterizing a class of agents (*i.e.* a system), shows self-averaging behavior when its coefficient of variation vanishes as the class population grows to infinity. This property provides us with a rationale and a justification for macroeconomics to be concentrated on the mean of variables (Aoki *et al.*, 2007). Otherwise, if the opposite property of non-self-averaging behavior holds true, mean-field interaction, as represented for instance by representative agent's responses, proves to be a very poor approximation of the whole complex web of interactions, and distributions matter:

> [...] non-self-averaging models are sample dependent, and some degree of impreciseness or dispersion remains about the time trajectories even when the number of economic agents go to infinity. This implies that focus on the mean path behavior of macroeconomic variables is not justified. It, in turn, means that sophisticated optimization exercises which provide us with information on the means have little value." (Aoki and Yoshikawa, 2007, p. 3–4)

Actually, if we look at empirical microeconomic distributions (for instance, personal incomes or firms' size), we discover that they are quite stable, showing typical and invariant functional forms across time and space. Hence, the non-self-averaging property seems to characterize relevant economic variables, and the argument above applies: means have little value and interactions among agents cannot be ignored or replaced by interaction among means.[33]

Once the representative (mean) agent is dismissed, in order to overcome the problem of multiple interactions one may choose different solutions, for instance by following some stochastic aggregation procedure. We find, however, that the availability of easily employable computational power allow us to adopt the simplest and straightforward bottom-up procedure consisting in simulating the behavior of each agent by means of agent-based techniques, and simply adding-up or averaging simulated individual levels in order to obtain aggregates. In other words, with this approach we do not need to aggregate at all, but we simply let every single agent to choose actions and to interact with each other, allowing both for within, between[34] and mean-field interactions.

---

[33] One must be honest: the self-averaging property is only a sufficient condition in order to rely upon mean values and, consequently, non-self-averaging does not imply their discard. However, non-self-averaging is sufficient to strongly distrust the neoclassical justification for the use of mean values and to open the path to AB models.

[34] By *within* and *between* class interactions we always mean non-mean-field, one-to-one interactions.

2.5 Simulation and Validation

Summarizing the theoretical architecture put forth so far, the *BAM* model is eventually defined in terms of a set of coupled difference equations describing the evolution over time of the state variables characterizing each agent. Couplings come from interactions of one sort or another. In general, due to its high dimensionality this system cannot be solved exactly, and the conditions for an exact aggregation conducive to a representative agent are not respected. The model therefore must be simulated at the computer. In other words, we ask a computer program to solve the system for us in a *specific* case, i.e. for a specific constellation of parameter values and initial conditions.

Before entering the simulation stage, therefore, the main modeling problem is the choice of parameter values and of initial conditions for state variables and populations' size and attributes. Such a choice is of course not independent from the empirical validation of the model, that is the capability of the model to reproduce some properly chosen stylized facts, both at the micro and at the macro level. Indeed, parameterization is guided by little else than this. Of course, the selection of the empirical evidence we use for comparison is crucial, as it amounts to defining the criteria against which the model is evaluated. Historical behavior itself passes through a process of analysis and simplification that leads to the identification of a set of *stylized facts*, which are generally defined in probabilistic terms. In the end, therefore, the model is evaluated according to the extent it is able to statistically replicate a set of selected stylized facts.

At the micro level, the main goal of any validation exercise is to assess the capability possessed by the model to replicate some stylized facts concerning statistical distributions of individual-level state variables – for instance, the right skewed distribution of firms' size or of the income distribution – or micro-level actual histories – for any firm in a given sample, the year-on-year growth of sales and capital accumulation. At the macro level, the main goal of validation is to assess whether the model is able to generate by means of bottom-up simulation procedures statistical aggregates which replicate some stylized facts concerning aggregate variables, such as GDP, aggregate unemployment or inflation. Sensible initial choices of parameters, guided mainly by reasonable approximations to well known stylized facts, should allow the model to replicate satisfactorily those empirical regularities.[35] Once a satisfying initialization choice has been defined, Montecarlo simulations can be run to check for the robustness of results as the parameter space is suitably explored.

Operationally, the whole process of validation is meant to investigate "how good" the model is.[36] Of course, an answer to this question cannot be unique, as

[35] Notice, however, that more sophisticated techniques for the choice of parameter values are also available (Bianchi *et al.*, 2008).

[36] Validation of ABMs is becoming one of the major points in the agenda of agent-based researchers. In her website, Leigh Tesfatsion maintains an entire section dedicated to this topic (http://www.econ.iastate.edu/tesfatsi/empvalid.htm).

it depends on the particular evaluation criterion we use, which in turn depends on the final goal of our analysis. Furthermore, as in all simulations, the BAM model requires an additional layer of evaluation referring to the validity of the simulator (i.e., the computer program used in simulation) with respect to the model (*program validity*).[37] Once the satisfaction of program validity has been verified, and the program has been checked to be bug-free, the stage of *model validity* is assured.

Following the formalization proposed by Marks (2007), as we let **R** be the observed real world output (prices, quantities, profits, investments, consumption and so on), and **M** be the model output, five general cases of goodness-of-fit are possible:

a) no intersection between **R** and **M** ($\mathbf{R} \cap \mathbf{M} = \varnothing$): the model is *useless*;
b) the intersection $\mathbf{R} \cap \mathbf{M}$ is not null: the model can display some real world phenomena but not others, and can exhibit behaviors that do not historically occur. The model is said to *be useful*;
c) **M** is a subset of **R** ($\mathbf{M} \subset \mathbf{R}$): the model is accurate, but *incomplete*;
d) **R** is a subset of **M** ($\mathbf{M} \supset \mathbf{R}$): the model is complete, but *inaccurate* (or *redundant*, since the model might tell something about what could yet happen in the world);
e) **M** is equivalent to **R** ($\mathbf{M} \Leftrightarrow \mathbf{R}$): the model is *complete* and *accurate*.

All in all, the model is said to be *useful* if it can exhibit at least some of the observed historical behaviors; to be *accurate* if it exhibits only behaviors that are compatible with those observed historically; and to be *complete* if it exhibits all the historically observed behaviors.

Having defined the relationship between the model and the real world system being modeled, it remains to be explicated the way in which a validation procedure can be operationally conducted. Looking at the main methodological aspects developed in this still young but burgeoning literature, one can stumble on different taxonomies that classify alternative empirical validation procedures according to different paradigms. The interested reader can find a comprehensive discussion in Fagiolo *et al.* (2007). In what follows, in particular in Chap. 4, we will refer to the classification originally employed by Leigh Testatsion,[38] that refers to the relationships between simulated and actual data. Accordingly, an agent-based model can be empirically validated in three different ways:

Descriptive output validation. The aim of descriptive output validation, also called ex-post validation, is to match computationally generated output against already available actual data. This kind of validation procedure is probably the most intuitive one and it represents a fundamental step towards a good model's calibration. Ex-post validation is based on several well-known parametric and nonpara-

[37] On these points, see Kleijnen (1998), Troitzsch (2004), Richiardi *et al.* (2006) and Fagiolo *et al.* (2007).

[38] See footnote 10.

metric statistical techniques, from sensitivity analysis to goodness-of-fit tests. Recently, Bianchi *et al.* (2007) have used microanalytic simulation techniques, also known as microsimulations, as a descriptive output validation tool. In particular, actual data at a starting point are used to initialize an agent-based model, continuously comparing simulation results with actual data as the simulation goes on. The parameters of the model can then be calibrated in order to minimize the distance between simulations' output and reality (Gilli and Winker, 2003).

Predictive output validation. Predictive output validation is related to matching computationally generated data against yet-to-be-acquired system data. Obviously, the main problem concerning this procedure is essentially due to the delay between the simulation results and the final comparison with actual data. This may cause some difficulties when trying to study long-time phenomena. Anyway, since prediction should be the real aim of every model, predictive output validation must be considered an essential tool for an exhaustive analysis of any model meant to reproduce reality. The main statistical techniques used in predictive output validation are based on forecasting and time series analysis.

Input validation. Input validation is meant to ensure that the fundamental structural, behavioral and institutional conditions incorporated into the model succeeds in reproducing the main aspects of the actual system. This is what we prefer to call ex-ante validation: the researcher, in fact, tries to introduce the correct parameters in the model before running it. The information about parameters can be obtained analyzing actual data, thanks to common empirical analysis. Input validation is obviously a necessary step one has to take to build up a reliable model. An example of input validation is presented in Vagliasindi and Cirillo (2009), where the main assumptions at the heart of several agent-based models of industrial organization are empirically tested using actual data.

A last issue we touch upon is the relationship between validation and calibration. While validation represents a set of techniques meant to verify if the model is able to reproduce the actual phenomena for which it has been designed within a satisfactory range of accuracy, calibration represents the ensemble of statistical techniques aimed at improving the precision of the parameters' values used in simulations, according to a backward process that flows from the model predictions and actual data towards the model parameters (Fox, 1989). From this point of view, calibration should be seen as an ameliorative development that logically follows validation: first one tests the goodness of fit of the simulation model with respect to actual data by means of a broad constellation of parameters, then – if the model is deemed satisfactory – one tries to improve its fitting by intervening on the precision of parameters.[39] Among the many calibration techniques available,

[39] Admittedly, the logical order between the validation and the calibration stages we propose is not universally accepted among the agent-based community. Richiardi *et al.* (2006), for instance, argue for putting calibration before validation, as they consider validation as the final step of a well-calibrated simulation model.

we argue that the most promising one for AB models is the *indirect inference* procedure put forth by Gourieroux and Monfort (1996). In a nutshell, indirect inference consists in a simulation-based method for estimating parameters whenever the likelihood function of the original model is not analytically tractable or too complex to be evaluated. Differently from other simulation-based methods, however, indirect inference is based on the introduction of a criterion function derived from an auxiliary model that does not need to be an accurate description of the data generating process.

Chapter 3
The *BAM* Model at Work

> The classical theorists resemble Euclidean geometers in a non-Euclidean world who, discovering that in experience straight lines apparently parallel often meet, rebuke the lines for not keeping straight–as the only remedy for the unfortunate collisions which are occurring. Yet, in truth, there is no remedy except to thro over the axiom of parallels and to work out a non-Euclidean geometry.
>
> JOHN M. KEYNES
> *The General Theory of Employment, Interest and Money*, p. 16

3.1 BAM at Work

In this chapter we develop a prototype bottom-up macroeconomic (BAM) model,[40] which epitomizes the key features at the root of a series of computational investigations of macroeconomic processes conceived as complex adaptive systems (CATS), as recently performed by our research group. Other exemplifications of the CATS approach can be found in Delli Gatti *et al.* (2005), Gaffeo *et al.* (2007) and Russo *et al.* (2007).

In Sect. 3.2 we list the main ingredients of the BAM framework: agents, markets and trading processes. In Sect. 3.3 we carefully describe the *sequence* of actions and interactions which occur in the economy under scrutiny. A pervasive and recurrent feature of this sequence is the *search* process which goes on in each of the market considered: households search for a job on the labor market and for consumption goods on the goods markets, while firms search for a bank loan on the credit market. Search is costly, so that each searching agent can visit only a finite number – i.e., a subset – of potential "providers": firms which provide job opportunities on the labor market, firms which offer consumption goods on the

[40] A streamlined version of the present model and a succinct discussion of its features can be found in Delli Gatti *et al.* (2008).

goods market, banks which provide loans on the credit market. Each period the identity of the (finite number of) providers the searcher can visit changes partially at random, so that the network structure is continuously evolving over time, even if the number of "links" (providers) per "node" (searcher) is constant.

All *matching* processes occur in a completely *decentralized* setting. In our framework there is not any centralized auctioneer at work, so that actual transactions can well occur at out-of-equilibrium prices. Moreover, we do not resort to any exogenous "matching function", a deterministic device which plays the crucial role of coupling agents on the two sides of the labor market in mainstream search-and-matching models of equilibrium unemployment. The main advantage of the BAM model is that one can directly simulate the above-mentioned myriad of dispersed interactions by means of an algorithmic representation, instead of recurring to an aggregate proxy of the behavior of customers trying to buy and of suppliers trying to sell. Sects. 3.4, 3.5 and 3.6 are therefore devoted to an in-depth discussion of the working of the search-and-matching processes in the market for labor services, for bank loans and for consumption goods, respectively.

In Sect. 3.7 we focus on the macroeconomic role of bankruptcy. Financial conditions of firms and banks, in fact, play a crucial role on all the markets considered, either directly or indirectly. When a firm's or bank's financial fragility reaches a critical point, i.e. when its net worth turns negative, that economic unit goes bankrupt. Bankruptcy therefore is the most straightforward device to introduce an *exit* mechanism in our virtual economy. An entry process occurs in parallel with exit, so that in our model firms' demography is fully taken into account.

The (baseline) model described so far is based upon the assumption of a *constant* labor productivity and is capable of reproducing the irregular "short run" fluctuations of aggregate output which is actually characterizing real world economies (as will be shown in Subsect. 3.9.1). In Sect. 3.8 we further introduce an endogenous mechanism for the determination of labor productivity, which links productivity to investment in R&D and the latter to profits. In this case it is easy to show that the model displays both growth and irregular fluctuations. This is the reason why we label this extension the "growth+" model.

Sect. 3.9 is devoted to an analysis of simulations' results. Since the empirical validity of a model can be assessed comparing theoretical predictions with a selected set of *explananda*, we believe that at least two issues are of key importance in evaluating the empirical success of the BAM model.

First of all, the BAM model should be able to replicate the tendency of the macroeconomy to *self-organize* most of the times, but also to occasionally display severe *coordination failures* so that, say, a great depression can occur because of the transmission of an idiosyncratic shock, i.e. in the absence of a major negative aggregate shock. Macroeconomic models of the usual sort, on the contrary, usually exhibit either regular behavior all the time (whenever a stable equilibrium exists), or permanent degenerate behavior (whenever the previous condition does not hold). In the standard literature the second scenario is discarded a priori so that (short-lived) fluctuations can occur only if an aggregate shock hits the macro-economy and displaces it from its stationary equilibrium.

Second, the BAM model should be able to replicate, at least qualitatively, one or more of the stylized facts of macroeconomic importance that are known to hold for most of the industrialized countries. In particular, we are interested in building a virtual environment able to capture the emergence of aggregate regularities as the result of decentralized interactions of a multitude of heterogeneous agents.

Notice that these criteria for the empirical corroboration of predictions from the BAM model are mainly *qualitative*. A different but complementary strategy consists in adopting *quantitative* methods for *ex-post validation*. We defer to Chap. 4 an exercise in ex-post validation of the model. In the rest of this chapter we focus instead on the qualitative measures just outlined, and in particular we assess the performance of the BAM model in producing:

- a non degenerate dynamics of the aggregate variable of interest (output) punctuated by sudden crises;
- emergent macroeconomic regularities, such as correlated paths of labor productivity and the real wage, Phillips and Beveridge curves and the Okun's law;
- co-movements among aggregate variables and leads-and-lags correlations.

Going to the details, in Subsect. 3.9.1 we discuss results concerning the baseline scenario, while Subsect. 3.9.2 is devoted to the output of simulations of the growth+ model. A check on the robustness of these findings as regards variations in the parameter constellation is postponed to Sect. 3.10. Before it, though, in Subsect. 3.9.3 we perform an assessment exercise by means of actual and simulated data in order to compare the BAM methodological approach to that currently used in modern macroeconomics (DSGE). Finally, Subsect. 3.9.4 describes one of the many possible extensions of the model, with the aim of showing the degree of flexibility of the BAM model.

We hope that the evidence reported in Sect. 3.9 and 3.10 will be sufficient to convincingly convey the belief that identifiable aggregate regularities consistent with the stylized facts may easily appear from the complex interactions of heterogeneous adaptive adjustments on different margins, technological innovation, limited search and out-of-equilibrium decentralized transactions on three interrelated markets.

3.2 The Environment

In order to build an agent-based model, three main ingredients are necessary.

1. The list of the *agents* that populate the model. Generally, pre-determined subsets of the population identify groups or *classes* of agents characterized by specific macroeconomic roles.
2. The *structure* of each agent, which consists of:
    - a list of the *state variables* that describe the agent in every period of the time horizon considered (which translates into a step of the simulation). The "snapshot" of the condition of the agent in a given period, i.e. the vector of

levels of the state variables concerning the specified agent in that period, is the *internal state* of the agent;
- a list of the possible *actions* (the levels of the control variables) that agents can perform. Actions will affect not only their internal state but also the internal state of other agents.

Agents belonging to the same class have the same macroeconomic role and have similar structures. They may be characterized, however, by a specific level of one or more microeconomic (state or control) variables. This allows to preserve individual specificity also within each class.

3. The network of interactions that links agents within the group and among groups. Among group interactions typically occur in virtual or geographically characterized markets.

As to point 1), our model describes a sequential closed economy populated by a finite number ($I + J + B$) of agents grouped into three classes:

- firms, indexed by $i = 1, \dots, I$;
- workers/consumers, indexed by $j = 1, \dots, J$;
- banks, indexed by $k = 1, \dots, K$.

As to point 2), each agent is characterized both by a set of state variables (e.g. productivity, net worth), and by a set of control variables (e.g. notional prices and quantities). Finally, as to point 3), agents undertake decisions at discrete times $t = 1, \dots, T$ on three markets:

- a market for a homogeneous non-storable consumption good;
- a market for labor services;
- a market for credit (bank loans).

Since agents' decision making processes are constrained by imperfect/incomplete information and by limited computational capabilities – a condition which can be labeled with the evocative term of bounded rationality (Simon, 1997; Kaneman and Tversky, 1981) – we assume that actions are not the outcome of an optimization process, but they are chosen *adaptively* according to rules of thumb buffeted by idiosyncratic random disturbances.

Markets are characterized by continuous decentralized search and matching processes (the so-called *procurement process* in the parlance of Tesfatsion [2005]), which imply individual, and *a fortiori* aggregate, out-of-equilibrium dynamics. Even in the absence of a centralized market-clearing mechanism, the economy shows a tendency to *self-organize* towards a *spontaneous order* which is however characterized, depending on the market and the time horizon, by persistent involuntary unemployment, unsold production or excess demands, and credit rationing. While in the standard macroeconomic theory these phenomena are treated as "pathologies" – i.e., departures from a first-best scenario due to imperfections of one sort or another –, in our framework they are emerging properties – i.e., "physiological" outcomes – of the macroeconomy.

The modeling strategy of the BAM framework is built on two pillars. First, the rules of individual behavior and market transactions (that we translate into algorithmic language) are inspired – whenever possible – to the evidence available from survey studies conducted by asking households and business people how they actually behave. Where several competing theories are available, we conform to the dull version of the Occam's Razor principle known as KISS.[41] Second, as discussed at length above, we do not impose any centralized solving mechanism. Instead, we let the system of adaptive interacting agents evolve autonomously towards self-organizing configurations: in other words, we will not impose the exogenous choice of any equilibrium, but we allow the endogenous *formation* of one of them, if it exists.

3.3 The Sequence of Events

The sequence of events runs as follows:

1. Each operating firm decides on the amount of output to be produced (hence, the amount of labor to be hired) and the price to be charged according to expected demand for consumption goods. Expectations of future demand are updated adaptively, i.e. they are formed on the basis of the firm's past experience.[42]
2. A fully decentralized labor market opens. Firms post their vacancies at a certain offered wage, and unemployed workers contact a given number of randomly chosen firms to get a job, starting from the one that offers the highest wage. Firms then have to pay the wage bill in order to start production. Labor contracts expire after a finite number of periods θ. A worker whose contract has just expired applies first to her last employer.

---

[41] Several interpretations of the acronym KISS circulate, most of them overlapping. The one we prefer is *keep it simple, stupid!*

[42] Behavioral rules represent by construction the process of *adaptation* of the agent's actions to changes of the environment. In a behavioral setting therefore expectations formation can be modeled quite straightforwardly as an adaptive scheme: Firms form expectations on future demand only on the basis of the past history of production (which is demand constrained). This adaptive mechanism is inefficient from a rational expectations (RE) viewpoint. In fact, if agents cast adaptive expectations, sooner or later they will incur in systematic errors. In a RE setting, on the contrary, agents are rational, i.e. they are able to elicit all the necessary information – not only the past history of the variable in question – and process it in such a way as to make only random errors which cancel out in the aggregate. Notice, however, that from the statistical point of view REs are conditional expectations of the system's data generating process (DGP). As such they are inherently liable to errors. In any given situation, according to the RE theory agents endowed with rational expectations should not make mistakes *on average*, but in practice they do. In order for agents to assess whether their specification of the DGP's conditional mean is right or not, the situation must be repeated over time in such a way as to allow agents to learn and update their expectation formation with the help of an "error correction" procedure. At the same time, however, the DGP is likely to change as well, frustrating agents' efforts to be "rational".

3. If internal financial resources (net worth) are in short supply with respect to the wage bill – i.e. if there is a financing gap – the firm can access a fully decentralized credit market. Borrowing firms contact a given number of randomly chosen banks to get a loan, starting from the one which charges the lowest interest rate. Each bank sorts the borrowers' applications for loans in descending order according to the financial soundness of firms, and satisfy them until all credit supply has been exhausted. The contractual interest rate is calculated applying a mark-up (which is itself a function of financial viability) on an exogenously determined baseline interest rate. After the credit market is closed, if financial resources – both internal and external – are not enough to pay for the wage bill of the population of workers, some workers remain unemployed or are fired.
4. Production takes one time period, regardless of the scale of production/firm's size.
5. After production is completed, the market for goods opens. Firms post their offer price, and consumers contact a given number of randomly chosen firms to purchase goods, starting from the one which posts the lowest price. If a firm ends up with excess supply, it gets rid of the unsold goods at zero costs. The good in fact is perishable and cannot be stored in a warehouse to be sold in the future.
6. Firms collect revenues and calculate gross profits. If gross profits are high enough, they "validate" debt commitments, i.e. firms pay back both the principal and the interest to the bank. If net profits are positive, firms pay dividends to the owners. In a "growth+" variant of the present model (to be discussed in Sect. 3.8), firms invest a fraction of net profits in R&D in order to increase their productivity before distributing dividends.
7. Earnings after interest payments and dividends are retained profits, which are employed to increase net worth. Net worth at the end of a period, in fact, is the sum of all retained profits accumulated in the past. Firms and banks are financially viable – and therefore survive – if their net worth is positive. If, on the contrary, net worth is negative, they go bankrupt, shut down and exit the market. Lenders, therefore, have to register a bad debt (non-performing loan).
8. A string of new firms/banks equal in number to the bankrupt ones enters the market. Their size at entry is smaller than the average size of exiting agents.

3.4 The Labor Market

The i-th firm carries on production by means of a constant return to scale technology, with labor L_{it} as the only input:

$$Y_{it} = \alpha_{it} L_{it}, \ \alpha_{it} > 0 \tag{3.1}$$

where α_{it} is labor productivity. While in this section productivity is considered as a parameter, in general it can change according to a simple rule of technological updating, which in turn depends on profitability and the availability of financial resources to carry on R&D expenditure. Heterogeneous financial conditions, therefore, imply heterogeneous productivity levels. The case of an endogenous, financially driven, productivity will be dealt with in the next section.

From equation (3.1), it follows that the desired workforce – i.e. the demand for labor, L_{it}^d, expressed as the number of workers the firm is allowed to hire – is simply given by:

$$L_{it}^d = \frac{Y_{it}^d}{\alpha_{it}}, \tag{3.2}$$

where Y_{it}^d is the desired level of production. In other words, the desired workforce represents the labor requirement that must be fulfilled to reach the desired scale of production. We will show in Sect. 3.6 how the latter is determined.

At the beginning of period t, each firm advertises the opening of vacant positions, and the associated offered wage. In order to determine the effective number of vacancies, note that at the beginning of period t the i-th firm is endowed with an *actual* workforce equal to $L_{it}^{\circ} = L_{it-1} - \hat{L}_{it-1}$, where L_{it-1} represents workers employed at the firm in (t – 1), while $\hat{L}_{it-1}$ is the number of workers whose labor contract has just expired. If the desired labor force is larger than the actual one, the firm creates a number of vacancies equal to $V_{it} = L_{it}^d - L_{it}^{\circ}$. Hence, the amount of open vacancies is:

$$V_{it} = \max\left(L_{it}^d - L_{it}^0, 0\right). \tag{3.3}$$

Workers with an active contract can be fired only if the firm's funds (both internal and external) are not enough to pay for the desired wage bill.

We assume that workers supply inelastically one unit of labor per period, and that only unemployed workers can search for a new job. In other words, we rule out on-the-job search. Each unemployed worker sends M applications to as many firms. If her contract has just expired, she applies first to the firm in which she worked in the previous period and, after that, she will send the remaining M–1 applications to as many firms chosen at random. New unemployed workers are therefore characterized on one hand by a sort of loyalty to their last employer, and on the other hand by a desire to insure themselves against the risk of unemployment by diversifying the portfolio of hiring opportunities. Of course, loyalty to the past employer does not make any sense if the worker has just been sacked, or if she has lost her job because of a bankruptcy. In all these cases, as well as when the worker is actually living a long spell of unemployment, she simply sends M applications to as many randomly chosen potential employers.

Once the offered contractual terms of vacant positions have been publicized to all applicant workers, each worker chooses to enter a settlement stage only with the firm offering the highest wage, out of the M firms she visited. Contracts are closed sequentially according to an order randomly chosen at each time step. Since each worker is allowed to sign one labor contract per period and the labor market microstructure is completely decentralized, serious "coordination failures" could arise due to two different reasons. First, the number of unemployed workers actually searching for a job in the aggregate does not necessarily correspond to the number of vacancies, so that aggregate excess supply or demand for labor is a frequent market outcome. Second, some firms – typically those that offer relatively high wages – may experience an excess of requests for employment with respect to actual vacancies, while some other firms – mainly those that post relatively low wages and hire workers late in the sequence – may end up in the opposite situations and some vacancies may remain unfilled.

When hired, a worker is asked to sign a contract that determines her nominal wage for a fixed number of periods. The contractual wage offered by firm i in period t is determined according to the following rule:

$$
\begin{aligned}
w_{it}^b &= \max\left(\hat{w}_t, w_{it-1}\right) \; \textit{if} \; V_{it} = 0 \\
w_{it}^b &= \max\left(\hat{w}_t, w_{it-1}\left(1+\xi_{it}\right)\right) \; \textit{if} \; V_{it} > 0
\end{aligned}
\tag{3.4}
$$

where $\hat{w}_t$ is the minimum wage (set by a mandatory law), while w_{it-1} is the wage offered to the cohort of workers employed the last time the firm hired. ξ_{it} is an idiosyncratic shock uniformly distributed on the interval $(0, h_\xi)$. The minimum wage is periodically revised upward, in order to catch up with inflation. In other words, wages are fully indexed. Wages set in the past that happen to fall below the current minimum wage are automatically aligned to the latter.[43] Workers paid the minimum wage therefore are fully insured against eroding purchasing power due to inflation. The indexation of the minimum wage may hamper the capability of firms to seek and preserve profitability, in a sort of wage-price spiral. For instance, in periods of *tight* labor market, firms that are expanding their workforce hiring new workers increase their price to preserve profit margins. Higher prices, in turn, drive the minimum wage up, offsetting the efforts of the firms. The process works in the opposite direction when the labor market is *loose*.

The design of the labor market we choose is somehow consistent with the findings reported by numerous surveys of firms' wage-setting policies. First, there is clear evidence of nominal wage downward rigidity. Firms are particularly reluctant to cut nominal wages even during recessions because they are afraid that lower wage rates would increase turnover and decrease labor effort (Campbell and Kamlani, 1997; Bewley, 1999). Second, downward rigidity is observed also for the salary of the newly hired workers, probably for reasons of perceived equity (Bewley, 1999). Akerlof and Shiller (2009) interpret this downward rigidity of the nominal wage as one instance of money illusion.

[43] In simulations we set the duration of contracts θ to 8 periods, while the minimum wage is revised every 4 periods. If we assume that one simulation period corresponds to a quarter, this means that labour contracts last two years, while the minimum wage is revised annually.

3.5 The Credit Market

At the beginning of period t, the generic firm i is endowed with an amount of retained past profits or net worth equal to A_{it} (see equation 3.12 below). If its desired wage bill W_{it} is larger than its net worth, the firm looks for a bank loan, $B_{it} = W_{it} - A_{it}$. The demand for credit therefore is simply given by:

$$B_{it} = \max\left(W_{it} - A_{it}, 0\right). \tag{3.5}$$

Due to transaction costs, the search for loans on the part of the firm is restricted: each firm can in fact apply for a loan only to a fixed number $H < K$ of banks. In a sense, if we extend to the credit market the conceptual apparatus originally introduced for the analysis of search and matching on the labor market, these are "credit applications" coming from agents in need of external finance.

Each time period t, the k-th bank will extend a total amount of credit C_k equal to a multiple of its equity base: $C_{kt} = E_{kt}/v$, where $0 < v < 1$ can be interpreted as a *capital requirement* coefficient. The reciprocal of v therefore represents the *maximum allowable leverage* for the bank. For simplicity, we assume for the moment that the capital requirement coefficient is determined by a regulatory authority, and is uniform across banks. If we apply to the credit market the conceptual apparatus we used for the analysis of search and matching processes in the labor market, C_k represents the amount of "credit vacancies" posted by the k-th bank.

Banks advertise credit opportunities consisting of credit vacancies and the associated "price", i.e. the nominal interest rate. We assume that a generic bank k offers to firm i a standard single-period debt contract, which defines an interest rate r_{it}^k and the corresponding repayment schedule:

$$\begin{matrix} B_{it}\left(1 + r_{it}^k\right) & \text{if} \quad A_{it+1} > 0 \\ R_{it+1} & \text{if} \quad A_{it+1} \leq 0 \end{matrix} \tag{3.6}$$

where R_{it+1} is the amount the bank succeeds in retrieving in case the borrower's net worth becomes insufficient, i.e. if the firm goes bankrupt. To be more precise, the contractual interest rate offered by bank k to firm i is determined as a mark-up over a policy rate set by the central monetary authority $\bar{r}$:

$$r_{it}^k = \bar{r}\left(1 + \phi_{kt}\mu\left(\ell_{it}\right)\right). \tag{3.7}$$

The mark-up is a function:

- of the specificity of the k-th bank, modeled as random variations in its operating costs and captured by the random variable ϕ_{kt}, an idiosyncratic shock uniformly distributed on the interval $(0, h_\phi)$;
- of the financial fragility of the borrower, captured by the term $\mu\left(\ell_{it}\right)$, $\mu' > 0$, where $\ell_{it} = \dfrac{B_{it}}{A_{it}}$ is the borrower's leverage.

The last term implies that the mark-up the bank charges over the policy rate reflects a risk premium increasing with the financial fragility of the borrower.

Equation (3.7) can be interpreted in the light of the theory of the "external finance premium" pioneered by Bernanke and Gertler (1989, 1990). In the presence of ex post asymmetric information and costly state verification, the higher the borrower's financial fragility, the more frequent the auditing activity of the bank should be, and the higher the interest rate charged to the borrower. Alternatively one can think of (3.7) as the reduced form of a model in which a commercial bank can insure against potential losses due to lending by borrowing, at least to a certain extent, from a central bank acting as a lender of last resort. The policy rate, in this case, is the rate at which the central bank refinances the commercial bank. A by-product of this interpretation is that in principle firms can always find external funds and can be credit rationed only when total credit supply is small (i.e. v is large), since banks can obtain additional funds from the central monetary authority and price-discriminate among borrowers, via interest rates, according to their quality.

A firm which needs external finance can explore a segment of the market for bank loans by randomly picking H banks out of the population of K banks. Once the terms of the credit opportunities at the H banks have been revealed, the firm chooses the bank offering the lowest interest rate. We assume that the demand for credit is divisible, so that if the most preferred bank is in short supply of credit the firm can resort to the remaining H–1 banks. If total resources are still not sufficient to pay for the wage bill, the firm will be allowed to fire redundant workers at zero costs.

Contract settlements are closed sequentially, according to an order randomly chosen at each time step. Since the credit market microstructure is completely decentralized, once again serious "coordination failures" could arise. First of all, the amount of credit demanded in the aggregate does not necessarily correspond to the credit supply. Second, some banks may experience an excess of demand for loans with respect to "credit vacancies" – generally those banks that post relatively low interest rates – while some other banks may end up in the opposite situation and some vacancies may remain unfilled, especially in the case of banks which post relatively high interest rates. Some firms will therefore be rationed.

3.6 The Market for Consumption Goods

At the beginning of each period, the i-th firm adjusts its control variables, i.e. the price or the quantity supplied, to adapt to changing business conditions. In spite of the good being homogeneous, asymmetric information and search costs imply that consumers may end up buying from a firm even if its price is not the lowest. It follows that the conditions for perfect competition are not satisfied, and the law of one price does not apply (Stiglitz, 1989). Each firm has a certain degree of market power on its own local market.

For simplicity, we assume that a firm can change either the price or the quantity, but not both of them at the same time. In other words, the strategies consisting in "changing the price" and in "changing the quantity" are mutually incompatible. This assumption is based on the evidence of survey data on price and quantity adjustment of firms over the business cycle (Kawasaki *et al.*, 1982; Bhaskar *et al.*, 1993).

For expositional simplicity we assume that each strategy is ex-ante equally likely. In principle, however, we could attach a probability to each strategy which could be calibrated on real data. For instance, the available evidence suggests that liquidity constrained firms – i.e. firms with a limited cash-flow – quantity adjustments are more likely during recessions than during booms, whereas the reverse is true for price adjustments; i.e. constrained firms are less likely to cut prices in recessions.

In our model, the adaptation of each strategy depends on signals coming from the internal condition of the firm and/or from the market environment. The information set relevant for price or quantity adjustment of the i-th firm at time t consists of two components:

- The level of excess demand/supply in the previous period. Excess supply is signaled by the accumulation of an inventory of unsold goods ($S_{it-1} > 0$). Since the good is perishable, this inventory cannot be carried over to t and therefore it is *temporary*. Moreover, we assume that the firm can get rid of the inventory at no cost. If demand happens to be equal to supply or if there is excess demand, there will be no inventory ($S_{it} - 1 = 0$). In the former case, in principle, the firm has an incentive to reduce the price or reduce the quantity – we will be more precise momentarily – while in the latter case there is room for a price increase or an increase in quantity. There is a lower bound to a reduction of the price which is represented by the minimum price the firm has to charge to cover average costs.
- The deviation of the individual price from the average price $P_{it-1} - P_{t-1}$ during the last transaction round. If this deviation is positive (negative), the firm recognizes that it is charging a price higher (lower) than its competitors and therefore may be induced to reduce (increase) the price or the quantity to avoid (facilitate) a massive migration of consumers in favour of (from) its rivals. Also in this case a reduction of the price is bounded from below: the price cannot be lower than the minimum price the firm has to charge to cover average costs.

Internal conditions (i.e. the level on the temporary inventory or the individual price) are private knowledge, while the aggregate price is common knowledge.

In principle we have four cases. As we said above, we assume that price changes and quantity changes cannot occur simultaneously. Therefore, we associate *either* a price change *or* a quantity change to each case.

a) In case inventories are positive (excess supply) and the individual price is high with respect to the average, the firm will reduce the price (until the lower bound is reached) keeping the quantity unchanged.
b) In case inventories are zero (excess demand) and the individual price is low with respect to the average, the firm will increase the price keeping the quantity unchanged.

c) In case inventories are positive (excess supply) and the individual price is low with respect to the average, the firm form an expectation of lower demand today (in t) than yesterday (in t–1) and therefore will reduce the quantity supplied keeping the price unchanged.

d) In case inventories are zero (excess demand) and the individual price is high with respect to the average, the firm forms an expectation of higher demand today than yesterday and will increase the quantity keeping the price unchanged.

In cases *a)* and *b)* the firm has an unambiguous incentive to change the price in the suggested direction. In case *c)* the firm could in principle cut the price to allure consumers instead of cutting production, but this move would reduce profitability. In case *d)* the firm could in principle increase the price to reduce demand instead of increasing production, but this move would induce a loss of customers. The strategy of changing prices in cases *c)* and *d)* moreover is based on the implicit assumption that the firm is able and willing to manipulate demand through price changes, a situation that we can rule out on the ground of bounded rationality.

Cases *a)* and *b)* are incorporated in the following price rule:

$$P_{it}^{s} = \begin{cases} \max[P_{it}^{l}, P_{it-1}(1+\eta_{it})] & \text{if } S_{it-1} = 0 \text{ and } P_{it-1} < P \\ \max[P_{it}^{l}, P_{it-1}(1-\eta_{it})] & \text{if } S_{it-1} > 0 \text{ and } P_{it-1} \geq P \end{cases} \tag{3.8}$$

where η_{it} is an idiosyncratic random variable uniformly distributed on the support $(0,h_\eta)$, and P_{it}^{l} is the lowest price at which firm is able to cover average costs:

$$P_{it}^{l} = \frac{W_{it} + \sum_{k} r_{kit} B_{kit}}{Y_{it}}. \tag{3.9}$$

Cases *c)* and *d)* trigger quantity adjustments. In this case, the level of production planned or "desired" at the beginning of period t (Y_{it}^{d}) is equal to expected demand, $Y_{it}^{d} = D_{it}^{e}$. Expectations on future total orders – and therefore the scale of production – are revised adaptively according to the following rule:

$$D_{it}^{e} = \begin{cases} Y_{it-1}(1+\rho_{it}) & \text{if } S_{it-1} = 0 \text{ and } P_{it-1} \geq P_{t-1} \\ Y_{it-1}(1-\rho_{it}) & \text{if } S_{it-1} > 0 \text{ and } P_{it-1} < P_{t-1} \end{cases} \tag{3.10}$$

where ρ_{it} is an idiosyncratic shock uniformly distributed on the support $(0,h_\rho)$. Thus, expectations are revised upward if a manager observes excess demand for its output and its price is already above the average price on the market, and downward when the opposite holds true.

The four cases and the associated adjustments are represented in Fig. 3.1. Point A is the "equilibrium" of the firm/market in this particular setting. It is characterized, on the one hand, by $P_{it} = P_t$. This means that all the agents charge

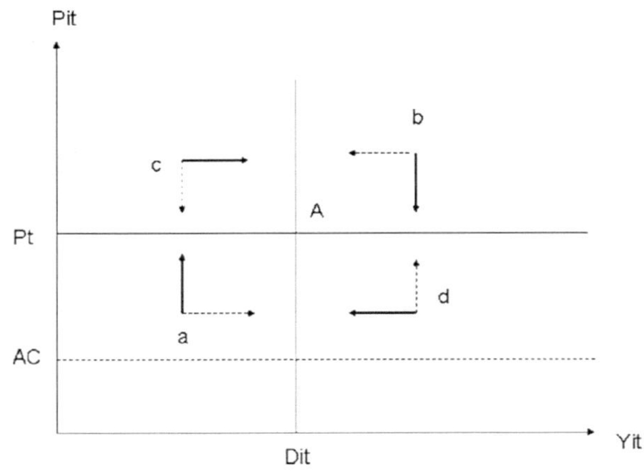

Fig. 3.1 Price and quantity adjustments for a generic firm *i*

the same price so that there is no incentive to change individual prices.[44] Moreover, $D_{it} = Y_{it}$, i.e. demand and supply are equal, so that involuntary inventories are equal to zero.

In the region characterized by *a)*, $P_{it} < P_t$ and $D_{it} > Y_{it}$ (i.e. $S_{it} = 0$): the firm has an incentive to increase the price (in order to catch up with its competitors) and, in principle, also an incentive to increase the quantity produced. In fact, since expectations are formed adaptively, the firm simply adds a stochastic increment to its current output level to determine the future expected level of demand: $D^e_{it+1} = Y_{it}(1+\rho_{it+1})$. There is room therefore for quantity adjustment.

We have assumed, however, a separation between the domains of quantity and price adjustments so that, *in this case*, we inhibit quantity adjustment. This is the reason why the horizontal arrow is dotted. By increasing the individual price today, in fact, the firm will lower demand in the future so that the absorption of the increased volume of output is not granted. The other three scenarios and the implied adjustments of prices and quantities can be inferred straightforwardly from the figure.

It is clear from the arrows that in a sense there is an implicit tendency for the firm to move towards an "equilibrium". Having inhibited some of the possible price or quantity adjustments, this tendency would be characterized by a spiraling pattern on the price-quantity space. We have implicitly ruled out therefore monotonic convergence, which would be a likely occurrence in case the dotted arrows were solid ones. Notice, however, that the "equilibrium" itself is changing over time.

Total households' income is the sum of the wage bill paid to workers employed in t and of dividends distributed to shareholders. Since profits are realized at the end of period t–1, accounting consistency implies that dividends also are distributed in that same period.

---

[44] In a monopolistic competition setting characterized by Bertrand competition, this would correspond to a Symmetric Bertrand-Nash Equilibrium.

The marginal propensity to consume out of labor income c is a decreasing function of worker's total wealth, defined as the sum of labor income plus all accumulated past savings, and is defined by the following:

$$c_{jt} = \frac{1}{1+\left[\tanh\left(\frac{SA_{jt}}{SA_t}\right)\right]^{\beta}}, \tag{3.11}$$

where SA_t and SA_{jt} are average and consumer j's actual savings, respectively. These savings, in turn, are due to a typical precautionary motive in the face of income uncertainty: households hold assets to smooth their consumption in case of unpredictable declines in income associated with spells of unemployment.

In line with the empirical evidence from the Consumer Expenditure Survey (Souleles, 1999), as well as with predictions from the theory of consumption under uncertainty (Carroll and Kimball, 1996), the marginal propensity c of our artificial consumers is assumed to decline with personal wealth.

Given the absence of any aggregate market-clearing mechanism, consumers have to search for satisfying deals on a fully decentralized goods market. The information acquisition technology affects the number Z of firms a consumer can visit without incurring transaction costs. In other words, transaction costs are equal to zero if the consumer does not cross the border of her local market of size Z, but they become prohibitively high as soon as a consumer tries to search outside it. In what follows, the identity of the Z firms associated to a generic consumer j at any time period t is determined by a combination of chance and deterministic persistence. The search mechanism in fact works as follows:

- Consumers enter the market sequentially, the picking order being determined randomly at any time period t.
- Each consumer j is allowed to visit Z firms to assess the price posted by each one of them. In order to minimize the probability to be rationed, she visits for sure the largest (in terms of production) firm visited during the previous round, while the remaining Z–1 firms are chosen at random. Thus, consumers adopt a sort of preferential attachment scheme, whereby preference is given to the biggest firms.
- Posted prices (and the corresponding firms) are then sorted in ascending order, from the lowest to the highest. Consumer j tries to spend a fraction c out of the labor income earned in period t–1 and of accumulated past savings in goods of the firm charging the lowest price in his local market.
- If the cheapest firm has not enough output to satisfy j's needs, the latter tries to spend her remaining income buying from the firm with the second lowest price, and so on.
- If j does not succeed in spending her whole income after she visited Z firms, she saves (involuntarily) what remains for the following periods. For the sake of simplicity, the interest rate on savings is assumed to be equal to 0.

The search and matching process described above is based upon an evolving network structure. The links connecting firms and consumers are in fact continuously changing over time. In particular, the mechanism that governs the choice of a seller on the part of the buyers yields a sort of *preferential attachment*. The firm which posts the lowest price in fact attracts a large fraction of consumers and crowds out competitors, gaining the ability to stay on the market in a predominant position also in the future. After the market for consumption goods has closed, the ith firm has sold Y_{it}, at the price P_{it}. Accordingly, i's revenues are $R_{it} = P_{it}Y_{it}$. Due to the decentralized buying-selling process among firms and consumers, it is possible that a firm remains with unsold quantities ($S_{it} > 0$). In the following period, the variable S will be used as a signal in adjusting firms' prices or quantities, as explained above.

3.7 Bankruptcy, Exit and Entry

At the end of period t, each firm computes profits $\pi_{it} - 1$. Should they be positive, firm's shareholders receive dividends $Div_{it} - 1$, which are calculated as a fixed fraction δ.

The residual, i.e. retained profits, are added to net worth inherited from the last period, A_{it-1}. Therefore, the law of motion of net worth of a profitable firm is:

$$A_{it} = A_{it-1} + \pi_{it-1} - Div_{i-1} \equiv A_{it-1} + (1-\delta)\,\pi_{it-1}. \tag{3.12}$$

As we have seen above, net worth is used to finance the wage bill. If internal funds are insufficient, firms can borrow external funds from banks.[45] The higher the amount of debt relative to net worth – i.e., the leverage ratio – a firm records, the higher is the probability of bankruptcy, *ceteris paribus*. If net worth turns out to be negative, i.e. if the firm records a loss (negative profit) and this loss is such as to wipe out all net worth accumulated in the past, the firm becomes technically insolvent and is declared bankrupt. In the case of the bankrupt firm – say firm f – therefore $\pi_{ft-1} < 0$ and

$$A_{ft-1} < -\pi_{ft-1}, \text{ so that } A_{ft} = A_{ft-1} + \pi_{ft-1} < 0. \tag{3.13}$$

As a consequence, the bankrupt firm exits the market. In line with a large literature on capital market imperfections, then, net worth is the key variable to assess the firm's viability. When a firm is not viable any more, i.e. when it goes bankrupt, it exits the market. For this reason, bankruptcy is the most straightforward mechanism to model exit. From the viewpoint of complexity, the dynamics of operating cash flows drives the selection mechanism.

[45] For simplicity, we assume that firms do not attempt to raise funds by issuing new equities. This admittedly extreme assumption can be grounded in asymmetric information on the stock market. The manager of the equity issuing firm, in fact, can assess the fundamental value of the firm much better than the potential shareholder and this asymmetric information scenario is common knowledge. In this setting *equity rationing* can occur, i.e. the firm may eventually rule out the issuing of new equities because the shareholders would purchase the new shares only at too low a price.

Of course, new firms are also entering the market. We assume that each bankrupt firm is replaced by a new entrant whose initial condition (size at entry) is set below the average size of incumbent firms.[46] This one-to-one replacement of bankrupt firms with entrant firms is essentially a working hypothesis, which allows us to keep the total firms' population constant. We can offer a rationale for the assumption, however, based on two widely accepted stylized facts (Sutton, 1997). First, in each established (mature) industry, there is a tendency for the number of firms to settle down around a roughly constant level, below the maximum recorded in that sector's history. Second, the inflow and outflow of firms are highly correlated: Geroski (1991), for example, reports a correlation coefficient of 0.796 for a sample of 95 industries in United Kingdom in 1987. Implicitly we are assuming a correlation equal to 1.

Due to firms' bankruptcies, banks will record non-performing loans (bad debt). Bad debt on the bank's book is equal to a certain share of the bankrupt firm's equity. For example, if the bank if financing 50% of firm's debt and the firm goes bankrupt, the bank will write down its assets' value for an amount equal to 50% of firm's equity. Consequently, a law of motion for banks' equity can be defined as well:

$$E_{kt} = E_{kt-1} + \sum_{i \in \Theta} r_{kit-1} B_{kit-1} - BD_{kt-1} \tag{3.14}$$

where Θ is bank k's loan portfolio, r_{kit-1} is the interest rate charged to firm i at time t–1 and $BD_{kt-1} \leq \sum_{i \in \Theta} B_{kit-1}$ represents bank's bad debt. As for firms, it may happen that bank's equity becomes negative. In this case the Government bails the bank out, replacing it with a random copy of surviving banks.

3.8 The "Growth+" Model: R&D and Productivity

A key insight of modern growth theory is that technological progress is an incentive-respondent activity pursued directly at the firm level. In this section we discuss a simple variation of the baseline framework to allow for the endogenous evolution of productivity, and we label this case the "growth+" scenario.

In order to implement this variant of the basic BAM model, we assume that productivity evolves over time according to a first-order autoregressive stochastic process:

$$\alpha_{it+1} = \alpha_{it} + z_{it} \tag{3.15}$$

where z_{it} is the realization of a random variable, exponentially distributed with parameter $\frac{1}{\mu_{it}} = \frac{p_{it} Y_{it}}{\sigma_{it} \pi_{it}}$. The parameter σ_{it} is the fraction of gross nominal positive

[46] To compute the average size of the incumbent firms we use the truncated mean at 10%. This means the lower and upper 5% of the firms' population are ruled out.

profits (π_{it}) which is used to fund investments in R&D. Hence, μ_{it} is R&D expenditure per unit of output, or R&D expenditure intensity. It follows that in our setting the higher R&D intensity is, the higher the expected increase in productivity results.

In simulations, σ_{it} will be modeled as an exponential function decreasing with the firm's financial fragility, defined as the ratio between the current wage bill and internal financial resources A_{it}, and normalized such that $\sigma_{it}(0) = 10\%$. As a consequence, fluctuations in R&D expenditure can be traced back either to changes in profits or to endogenous changes in the behavioural parameter σ_{it}. Equation (3.15) and the operational underlying assumptions can be thought of as a reduced form reflecting theoretical and empirical considerations suggested by a profusion of studies on the determinants of corporate R&D investment (Reynard, 1979; Fazzari and Athey, 1989, Greenwald *et al.*, 1990), according to which investment in research activity for the sake of technical progress is inversely related to financial fragility.

In the "growth+" model the law of motion of net worth (3.12) must be amended to take into account not only the payment of dividends, but also R&D expenditures:

$$A_{it} = A_{it-1} + (1 - \sigma_{it-1}) * (1 - \delta)\pi_{it-1}. \tag{3.16}$$

In terms of the computational model, the growth mechanism can be switched off by simply posing the parameter $\sigma = 0$ for all firms.

3.9 Simulation Results

We are now ready to explore the key properties of the BAM model. We run several sets of simulations using the constellation of parameters presented in Table 3.1. The choice of parameter values has been constrained merely by the need to rule out patently unrealistic dynamic behavior, i.e. degenerating paths identifiable by visual inspection and conventional empirical standard.[47] In particular, no attempt has been made at this stage to calibrate the model – for instance, by means of genetic algorithms – in order to force the output of simulation to replicate some pre-selected empirical regularities. As we will see momentarily, in spite of this limitation the model works pretty well along several margins. An analysis of robustness to changes in parameters through Montecarlo methods will be carried out in Sect. 3.10.

---

[47] Examples of degenerate dynamics we want to avoid are extremely volatile aggregate GDP dynamics, average rates of bankruptcy and unemployment over 50%, and average rates of annualized inflation outside the ±10000% range.

Table 3.1 Parameter values used in simulations

	Parameter	*Value*
I	Number of consumers	500
J	Number of firms	100
K	Number of banks	10
T	Number of time periods	1000
c_P	Propensity to consume of *poorest* people	1
c_R	Propensity to consume of *richest* people	0.5
σ_P	R&D investment of *poorest* firms	0
σ_R	R&D investment of *richest* firms	0.1
h_ξ	Maximum growth rate of wages	0.05
H_η	Maximum growth rate of prices	0.1
H_ρ	Maximum growth rate of quantities	0.1
H_ϕ	Maximum amount of banks' costs	0.1
Z	Number of trials in the goods market	2
M	Number of trials in the labor market	4
H	Number of trials in the credit market	2

3.9.1 The Baseline Scenario

We first simulate a baseline version of the model obtained by switching off R&D expenditure – i.e., $\sigma_P = \sigma_R = 0$ – so that productivity is constant. In the four panels of Fig. 3.2 we present the output of a representative simulation concerning: (*a*) the (log) real GDP; (*b*) the rate of unemployment; (*c*) the annual inflation rate and *(d)* the ratio of labour productivity to the real wage. In order to get rid of transients, only the last 500 simulated periods have been considered.

The time path of aggregate activity is characterized by irregular fluctuations around a roughly constant mean. The model is able to generate an alternation of booms and recessions as a non-linear combination of *idiosyncratic* shocks affecting individual decision-making processes. The account of business cycles offered by the present model is at odds with that provided by DSGE models, according to which fluctuations in aggregate activity are explained by random changes in *aggregate* variables such as TFP growth (as in RBC-DSGE models) or monetary, investment or mark-up shocks (NK-DSGE approach).

Sudden, deep and rather short recessions are due essentially to the bankruptcy of big firms, which spread through subsequent shockwaves to the economy as a whole. In fact, the bankruptcy of a firm, say α, yields:

- A negative *demand spillover*. The loss of employment generated by the failure of firm α, in fact, brings about a reduction of demand – financed out of the wages previously paid to α's workforce – for the products of other firms, say β and γ. These firms will experience a reduction of sales and, other things being equal, of profits. The accumulation of net worth of forms β and γ, therefore, will slow down and their fragility (and vulnerability to idiosyncratic shocks) will in principle increase.

- A *non-performing loan.* The bank which has extended loans to α will record a bad debt on its balance sheet. The accumulation of net worth at the bank, therefore, will slow down and the supply of loans will change in the same direction due to the target capital requirement ratio. This means that also β and γ may eventually face a constraint on the amount of credit they can get from the bank.

Even though we have not made any serious attempt at calibration, the BAM framework displays neither pathological phenomena, nor degenerate dynamics. The unemployment rate ranges between 2% and 12%, while the yearly rate of inflation is on average equal to 5%, and turns occasionally into moderate deflationary episodes. The average real wage and labour productivity follow a similar pattern so that – as shown in panel (*d*) – their ratio settles around a long run constant value of approximately 2/3. Since we did not impose any aggregate equilibrium relationship between the two variables, the (average) constancy over time of income shares turns out to be an emerging feature of our self-organizing system of heterogeneous interacting agents.

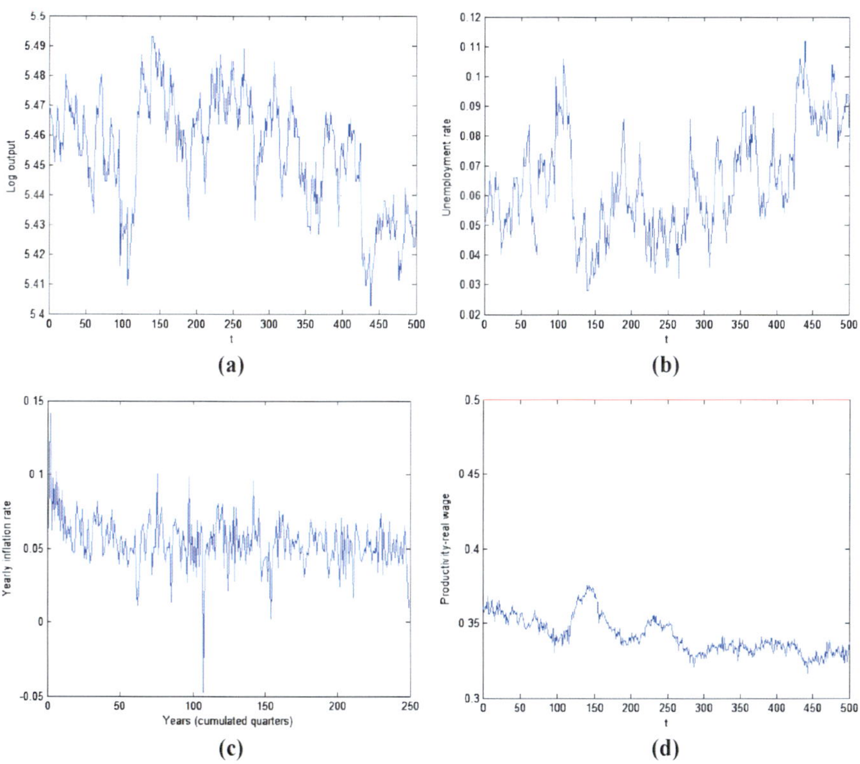

Fig. 3.2 Emergent macroeconomic dynamics from a representative simulation of the baseline model. (**a**) Real GDP; (**b**) rate of unemployment; (**c**) annualized rate of inflation; (**d**) productivity/real wage ratio

Other interesting aggregate stylized facts emerging from simulated decentralized interactions are shown in the four panels of Fig. 3.3. Panel (*a*) illustrates the presence of a negative relationship between the rate of wage inflation and the rate of unemployment, i.e. a standard (albeit quite flat) Phillips curve. The negative correlation between the two variables is weak (–0.10) but statistically significant. Panel (*b*) shows a negative relationship between the output growth rate and the unemployment growth rate – i.e. a typical Okun curve. A third emerging regularity regarding the labour market is the Beveridge curve reported in Panel (*c*), in which it is shown that a negative relationship appears as we plot the rate of vacancies (here approximated by the ratio between the number of job openings and the labour force at the beginning of a period) against the rate of unemployment. Also in this case the goodness of fit is not particularly satisfactory, but the negative correlation between the two variables, albeit weak (–0.27), is once again statistically significant. Finally, Panel (*d*) shows the firms' size distribution, with size measured by total production. As in the real world, the distribution is highly skewed to the right: small and medium sized firms dominate the economy; large firms are relatively rare, but their production represents a large part of total supply.

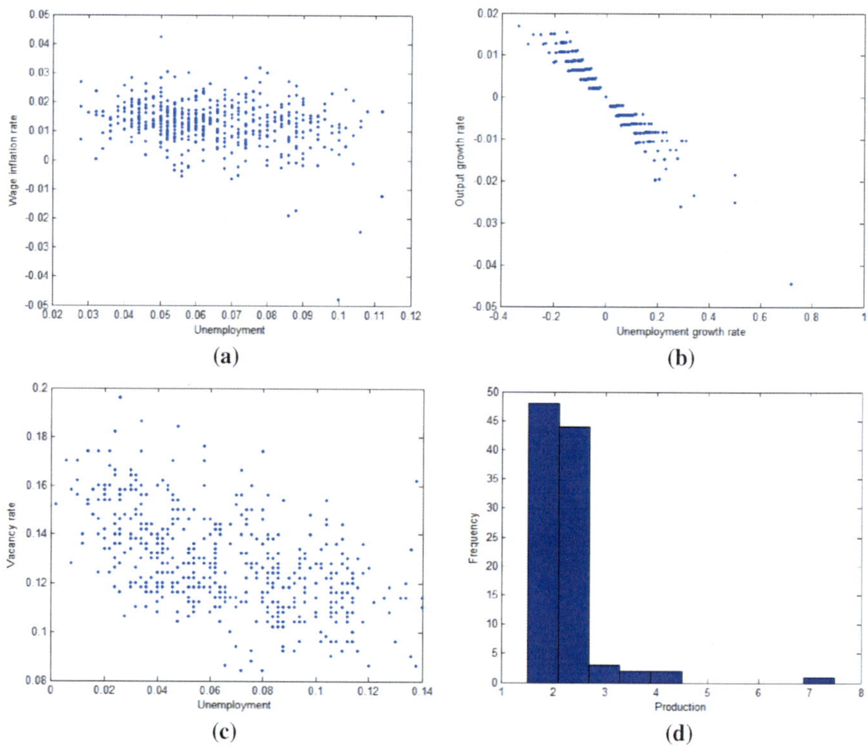

Fig. 3.3 Emergent macroeconomic dynamics from a representative simulation of the baseline model. Phillips (**a**), Okun (**b**) and Beveridge (**c**) curves, and the firms' size distribution (**d**) generated by simulations

3.9.2 *Profits, R&D and Productivity*

In this subsection we present results for the "growth+" version of the model, in which firms invest in R&D (σ_R >0), so that productivity evolves over time as described in Sect. 3.7. In Fig. 3.4 we present simulation results on the dynamics of GDP, the rate of unemployment, the rate of inflation, the productivity of labour and the real wage.

The main difference between this scenario and the baseline one (Fig. 3.1) is the time path of aggregate activity, which is now characterized by an alternation of aggregate booms and recessions along a *long-run* growth path. The reason for this dynamic pattern is obvious. Output growth is now driven by productivity growth stochastically depending on R&D investments. The latter, in turn, depend on the firms' financial conditions: the higher profits, the greater expenditure in R&D and the quicker the pace of productivity. As regards fluctuations, inflation, unemployment, productivity and the real wage, what we said about the baseline scenario applies here as well. Sudden stops of growth and short recessions are due essentially to the bankruptcy of large firms, which spread through the macroeconomy as

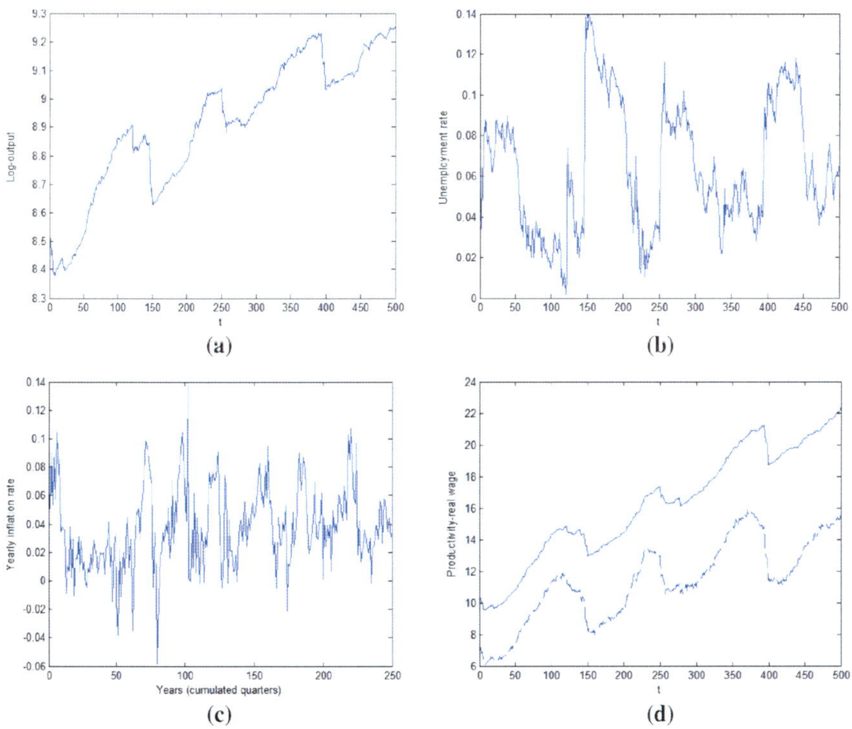

Fig. 3.4 Emergent macroeconomic dynamics from a representative simulation of the "growth+" model. (**a**) Real GDP; (**b**) rate of unemployment; (**c**) annualized rate of inflation; (**d**) productivity/real wage ratio

explained in the previous subsection. If we let each simulated time period correspond to one quarter, in our simulations the per-year probability to experience an economic disaster (i.e., a drop in real GDP of 15% or higher) is ranging between 0.8% and 1.7%. These figures are essentially in line with estimates reported by Barro (2006), according to whom the per-year probability of a big depression in OECD countries in the 100 years immediately before the global recession of 2008/09 is in the range 1.5–2%. Notice, however, that Barro includes wars into his calculation of major disruptions. Furthermore, in line with the long-run experience of industrialized countries, simulated data suggest that great depressions represent transitory disturbances, in that the long-run real GDP growth path is not significantly affected by major displacements.

Simulations illustrate that the likelihood and severity of economic disasters are increasing with the relevance assigned to the preferential-attachment scheme followed by consumers when searching for the best bargain in the goods market (see above, Sect. 3.6). This makes sense: if customers spread more equally over the market, the probability of finding a really big firm – and *a fortiori* the probability of finding a really big firm on the verge of bankruptcy – is lower. In fact, a preferential attachment scheme generates *auto-catalyticity*, a property a simple unit possesses whenever the time variations of the quantities characterizing it are proportional (via stochastic factors) to their current values. The performance of the macro system is then dominated by the micro units which happen to experience the highest auto-catalytic stochastic positive and/or negative growth rate, rather than by the behavior of a typical or *representative* element. The system is endowed with a kind of multiplier, which accelerates both positive and negative growth.

In Fig. 3.5 we present the Phillips, Okun and Beveridge curves emerging from the simulation of the "growth+" variant. Panel (*a*) shows the emergence of a Phillips curve. The negative correlation between the rate of wage inflation and the unemployment rate is small (−0.19), but statistically significant. Panel (*b*) shows the Okun curve. The Beveridge curve is reported in Panel (*c*): also in this case the goodness of fit is not that high, but the negative correlation between the two variables is statistically significant. Finally, Panel (*d*) shows the firms' size distribution. The shape of the latter is highly skewed to the right, as in the corresponding panel of Fig. 3.3.

In addition to the features characterizing the size distribution, a significant body of empirical literature (see e.g. Amaral *et al.,* 1997; Bottazzi and Secchi, 2005) has revealed that the observed distribution of firms' growth rates is tent-shaped and can be well represented by an asymmetric Laplace (i.e. double exponential) distribution. Though in general the theoretical functional form is excessively regular to capture empirical extreme values, which are generally distributed around much fatter tails than predicted by a Laplace, nonetheless the latter returns an extremely good fit in central portions of the data support.

Fig. 3.6 allows us to visually assess the ability of simulated data in replicating this empirical regularity. If we focus on the cross-sectional outcome in the last simulation period, the (log)rank-output growth rate (Panel *a*) is clearly tent-shaped for the bulk of the distribution, while both tails happen to be sensibly

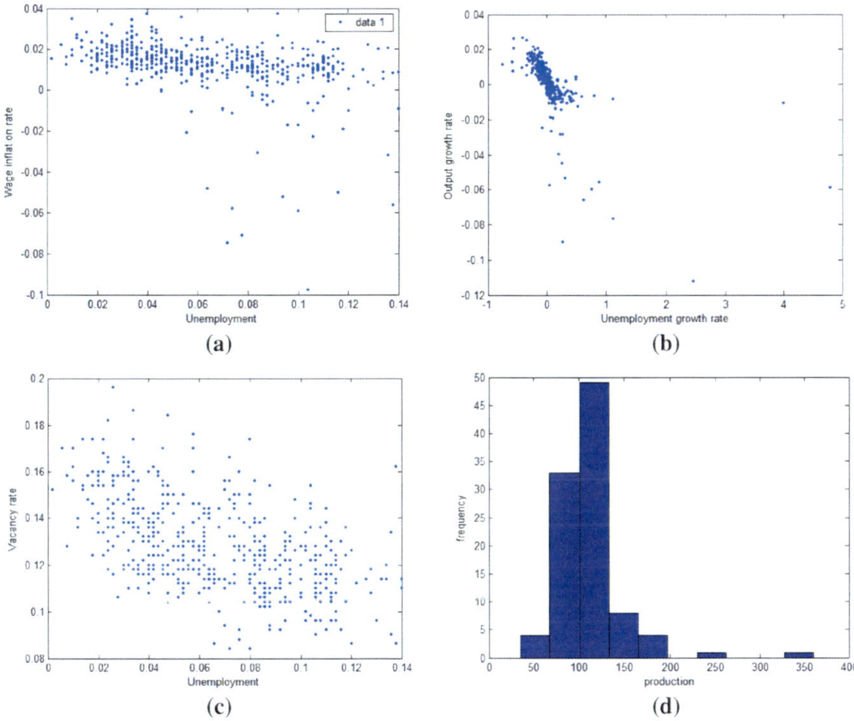

Fig. 3.5 Emergent macroeconomic dynamics from a representative simulation of the "growth+" model. Phillips (**a**), Okun (**b**) and Beveridge (**c**) curves, and the firms' size distribution (**d**) generated by simulations

fatter than predicted by the Laplace model. Furthermore, this regularity is robust to a change in the variable used to measure firms' size: a similar pattern emerges for the (log)rank-size diagram of the growth rate net worth (Panel *b*). The last two panels of the figure report simulated evidence for two additional aggregate variables: the average real interest rate (Panel *c*) and the number of firms which go bankrupt each period (Panel *d*). Their low-frequency fluctuations are clearly synchronized, as both of them peak in correspondence of aggregate slumps, a point which deserves to be further explored.

We start by observing that in this framework a recession is first and foremost the outcome of a wave of bankruptcies. The dynamics of aggregate economic activity is due to the combination of exogenous small idiosyncratic shocks, on the one hand, and of the endogenous systemic evolution stemming from the complex interaction of the financial stance of individual firms and the market structure, on the other one. All decisions regarding production plans are influenced by changes in financial positions: in a deep sense, we might say that business cycles are endogenous and financially-driven. Because of the stochastic nature of firms' productivity and the time-varying composition of the corporate sector, the frequency and amplitude of business fluctuations change over time; accordingly, the rela-

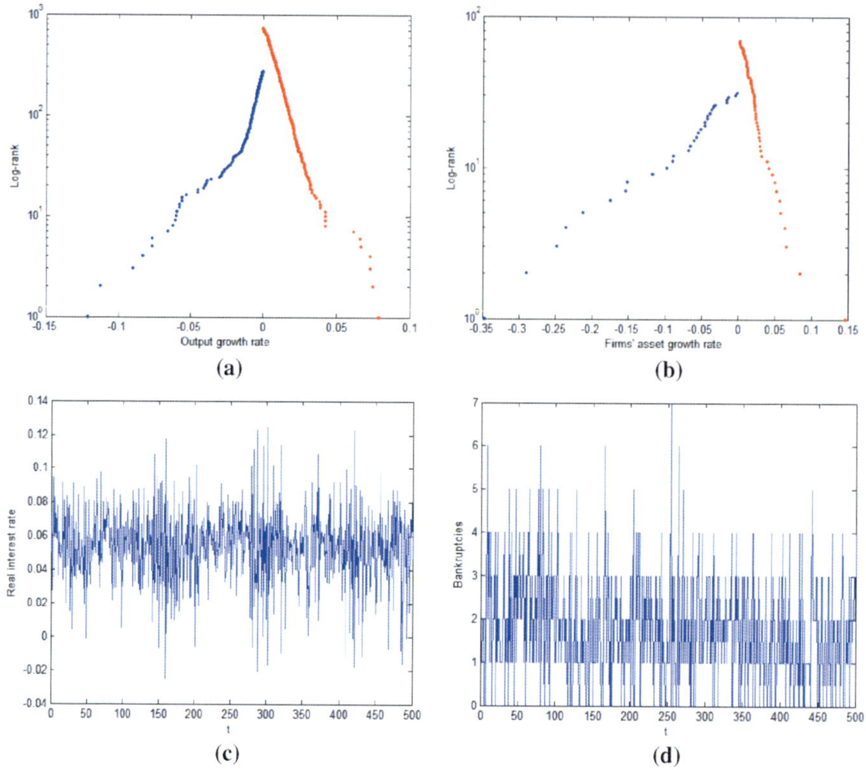

Fig. 3.6 Emergent macroeconomic dynamics from a representative simulation of the "growth+" model. (**a**) Distribution of output growth rates; (**b**) distribution of firms' net worth growth rate; (**c**) average real interest rate; (**d**) number of firms' defaults

tionship between the aggregate output and some measure of financial fragility (here, the cross-sectional average of wage-bill/total-equity ratios), though preserving over time the same qualitative pattern, changes from cycle to cycle. In particular, the endogenous nature of fluctuations can be described in terms of Hyman Minsky's "financial instability" hypothesis (Minsky, 1982), according to which a crisis is the result of two contextual tendencies. First, during expansions economic units tend to increase the risk embedded in their balance sheets, as they shift their liability structures from a hedge (units which can fulfill all of their contractual payment obligations by means of cash flows) to a speculative (units that can fulfil their payment obligations on "interest account", but cannot repay the principle out of cash flows) or even to a Ponzi (units whose cash flow is not enough to fulfill either the repayment of principle or the interest due on outstanding debts) position. Second, as the weight of speculative and Ponzi financing increases, the system as a whole becomes more and more sensible to falls in profits and to rises in interest rates.

The whole story can be appreciated by looking at Panel (*a*) of Fig. 3.7. The inception of big recessions – here signaled by shaded vertical areas – is in general

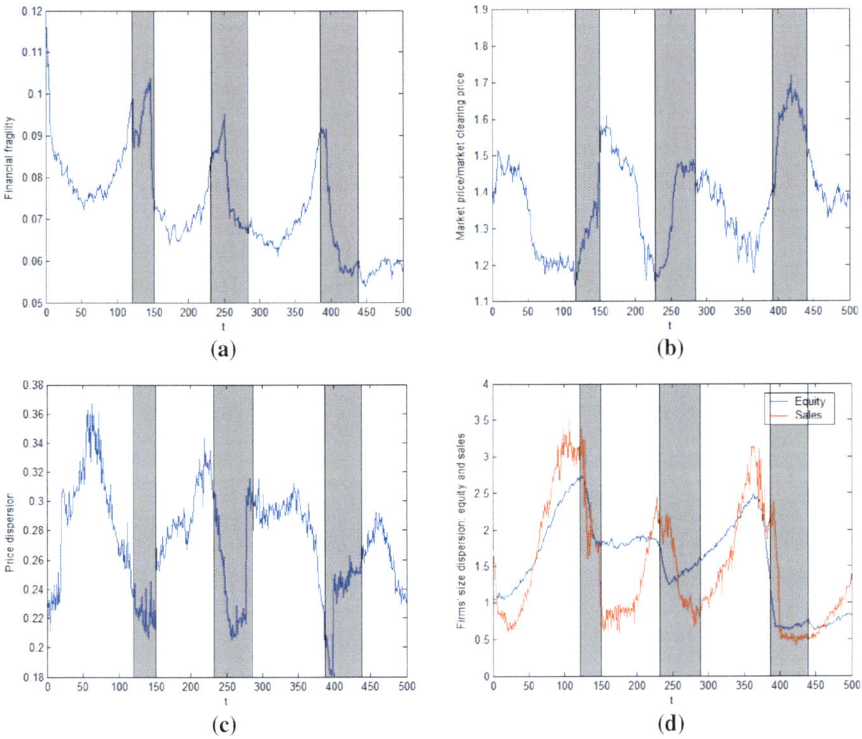

Fig. 3.7 Recessions (grey bands) and market structure from a representative simulation of the "growth+" model. (**a**) Financial fragility measured by the 'wage-bill to equity' ratio; (**b**) ratio between the market price and the market-clearing price; (**c**) firms' heterogeneity measured by the coefficients of variation of posted prices; (**d**) dispersion of the equity and sales distributions

heralded by a substantial increase of the cross-section mean leverage ratio, which decreases as the downturn ensues. During expansions, in turn, the financial fragility goes through two phases: it goes down steadily at first, to subsequently increase at an accelerating pace.

In an attempt to provide a chronological description of the intertwined dynamics of financial fragility and aggregate output during a financially-driven business cycle, we identify four different phases for any cyclical movement from trough to trough. The system goes through two distinct stages as the economic activity moves from a cyclical trough up to a peak along an expansion – a *period of tranquillity* (or *financially-hedge* phase) and a *financially fragile boom* period – and two distinct stages as the economy moves along a recession from a cyclical peak down to a trough, namely a *speculative recession* period and a *safe recession* (or *hedge depression)* period.

At the bottom of the cycle – i.e., at the lower turning point – the average debt-to-equity ratio is on a descending gradient, as the cascade of bankruptcies characterizing the now-ending recession has already "cleared up" the corporate sector, forcing all financially unsound (Ponzi) firms to exit the market. As the balance sheets of survivors become more and more robust due to such a natural selection mechanism, output and profits increase, while debt commitments become lighter. This scenario describes a virtuous circle – thus, a *period of tranquillity* – in which the growth of output and profits is paralleled by a decline of debt.

Positive profit opportunities tend to reduce risk-awareness, inducing firms to expand their production and to increase their workforce, generating positive demand spillovers and making their demand for external finance stronger. As a result, debts in the aggregate start increasing, and their escalating amount eventually determines a transition towards a *financially fragile boom* period, characterized by high leverage ratios and a growing sensitivity of firms' balance sheets to accidental falls in profits or increases in interest rates. The aggregate economic activity reaches its cyclical peak when the deterioration of individual balance sheet positions is such that a *normal* flow of idiosyncratic shocks starts transforming the rising number of speculative firms into Ponzi units, so that a higher-than-usual number of Ponzi units fail. This leads to an endogenous downturn, triggered by a new cascade of bankruptcies. A new recession begins.

Right after the upper turning point – during the *speculative recession* period – the sharp decline in profits starts to depress output and productivity growth. Firms' financial conditions are still unsound, and their debt-to-equity ratio goes further up. Only when the average financial soundness improves due to exists (bankruptcies) and deleveraging – i.e., when the debt-to-profit ratio starts declining – the recession becomes *safe* or financially robust. At the end of the robust depression, profits becomes greater than debt commitments, a turning point in the business cycle occurs and a new recovery sets in.

If we employ in our artificial world the Minsky's taxonomy of firms as regards their financial conditions, we find that in each simulated period approximately two thirds of the firms are hedge, while Ponzi firms represent less than one tenth of the whole population. Of course, the remaining units are speculative. While the ratio of the number of financially fragile (the sum of speculative and Ponzi) firms to that of hedge ones is rather stable over time, the cross-section mean of debt-to-equity ratios (that is, *systemic* financial fragility) is significantly pro-cyclical. This apparent inconsistency can be solved as one thinks about the role heterogeneity plays in our artificial world: during periods of positive growth some really big firms emerge, as suggested by a proxy of the market concentration index (Panel (*d*)). Even though the number of financially fragile firms is moderately stable over time, average fragility can go up as the economy expands simply because the financial position of a small number of very large firms eventually starts to become more and more unsound. Thus, our model corroborates the prediction of a substantial increase of overall financial fragility during "prosperous times" (the ascending phase of the business cycle), which is generally seen as the cornerstone of the financial instability hypothesis. Furthermore, unforeseen disturbances will trickle down across the whole distribution of agents because of aggregate demand spillovers, modifying this way the macroeconomic behavior. If composition effects are large enough, the response of the system to an identical shock changes over the business cycle, as it depends on the actual distribution of firms in terms of the balance between their internal and external finance.

Given that the degree of competition among firms and the distribution of profit opportunities interact with the dynamics of systemic financial fragility, an additional issue worth exploring is the evolution of market power over the cycle. As an indicator of market structure we employ the ratio of the actual (average) price index to the (homogeneous) equilibrium price, defined as the price that an imaginary Walrasian auctioneer would cry in order to equate the quantities demanded by households and supplied by firms (Panel (*b*)). An increase of the ability to price profitably above the competitive level – an increase of the value of the ratio depicted in Panel (*b*) – translates into an increase of market power. Over a typical cycle, the latter crosses three different phases. During a *robust expansion*, competition is becoming more and more fierce and actual price(s) tend to converge towards the market-clearing level. Such a convergence reaches its lower limit – with the actual-clearing price ratio remaining well above 1 – as the system enters a *fragile expansion*. It is only after a new recession sets in that individual prices start again to wander away from the fictitious Walrasian equilibrium level, as a stream of new bankruptcies shakes the market and the competitive pressure decreases accordingly. This in turn lowers significantly the standard deviation of prices (Panel (*c*)).

A somewhat opposite dynamics can be detected as regards the degree of heterogeneity of active firms, measured both in terms of their level of equity (net worth) and of sales. As depicted in Panel (*d*), during upswings dispersion increases steadily because the system dynamics is dominated by the micro units which happen to experience the highest stochastic autocalityc growth rate, and can grow very rapidly. On the contrary, during recessions dispersion reduces, as a certain number of large financially fragile firms are forced to exit due to bankruptcy, just to be replaced by new entrants characterized by a relatively homogeneous initial size.

3.9.3 Measuring the Performance of the BAM Model by Means of DSGE Methodology

Standard macroeconomic theory faces enormous difficulties in jointly explaining the rich list of phenomena we have just overviewed. For instance, basically all mainstream theories attempting to explain the Great Depression which hit the world economy during the 1929–39 period treat this episode basically as an outlier, and rely on a rather ad-hoc combination of severe frictions, technological and policy shocks to explain it (Chary *et al.*, 2002). BAM models, on the contrary, can naturally accommodate the alternation of phases of smooth growth and deep crises as instances of the same underlying dynamical process. For instance, in Panel (*d*) of Fig. 3.6 one can appreciate that the time series of firms' bankruptcies remains roughly constant during the whole simulation, even when the system experiences severe breakdowns. This feature of the model reveals the importance of heterogeneity, since a recession does not depend on the mere number of bankrupt firms but on their size: the same economic process can thus produce small or large recessions according to the size of bankrupt firms.

It must be noticed, however, that an appropriate comparison between the BAM family of models and more traditional DSGE models can be made only if a common testing methodology is employed. According to DSGE scholars, the explanatory performance of business cycle models has to be measured in terms of their ability to replicate aggregate phenomena at cyclical frequencies along three dimensions: persistence, volatility and co-movements of key variables with aggregate output. In this section we explore the ability of the BAM virtual economy to challenge DSGE models by mainly focusing on the latter dimension.

In particular, to make a more direct comparison we stick to qualitative measures of success. This could sound odd, since DSGE models are usually taken to the data by comparing quantitative theoretical predictions with figures summarizing key features of cyclical fluctuations in real economies. This impression is largely false, however. Since none formal metric is in general offered to measure the closeness of the model data to the real data, the assessment presented in almost every DSGE paper is ultimately qualitative. Hence, instead of reproducing the familiar table of figures based on actual and simulated data, we prefer to illustrate the performance of our BAM model in replicating first-order features of real economies with graphical methods.

For easiness of comparison with a conspicuous literature, the empirical benchmark used against simulation outcomes is the postwar U.S. economy. In particular, filtered-detrended quarterly data for real GDP, employment, labour productivity, real wages, inflation and bank loan interest rates obtained from the Federal Reserve web-based FRED© database have been used to calculate correlations at different leads and lags. Results are reported in the first five panels of Fig. 3.8, where we plot the cross-correlations with output at four leads and lags of: (*a*) employment, (*b*) labour productivity, (*c*) the price index, (*d*) the interest rate on loans and (*e*) the real wage. Each panel is completed by the corresponding function calculated from real data and a ±20% band, which is conventionally assumed as signaling a lack of correlation.

Our model does a remarkably good job in four cases out of five. From simulations we find that employment and productivity are highly correlated with contemporaneous output; prices are slightly negatively correlated and anticipate output; while the interest rate is a-cyclical. All these patterns mimic the evidence for the U.S. economy remarkably well. The simulated real wage turns out to be procyclical, as in real data, but fails to anticipate cyclical movements of aggregate activity by two to three quarters. Finally, Panel (*f*) presents the transitory impulse-response functions, calculated by means of an AR(2) estimate, for the actual (solid line) and the model-generated (dashed line) output, respectively. The simulated model can mimic the hump-shaped response of cyclical output to transitory

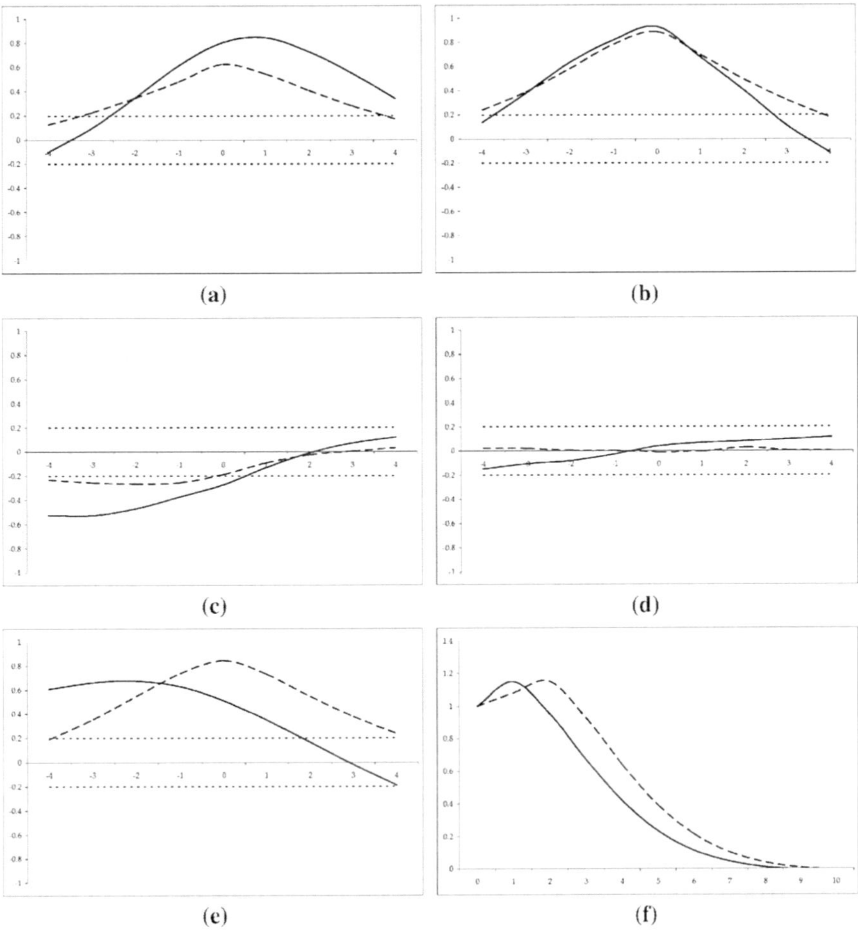

Fig. 3.8 Cyclical features of model-generated and real data. Solid lines show sample moments, while dashed lines show moments generated by simulations. (**a**) Employment; (**b**) productivity; (**c**) price index; (**d**) interest rate; (**e**) real wage; (**f**) GDP cyclical component impulse-response function

shocks – a feature that first-generation RBC models failed to capture (Cogley and Nason, 1995) – thought the peak in real data anticipates the simulated one by one quarter. The trend-reverting dynamics is nevertheless really similar.

Recalling that all these results have been obtained without any serious effort to properly calibrate the model, we argue that the BAM basic setup proves to display rich and interesting aggregate and disaggregated dynamics under rather general conditions. Furthermore, as we have just showed it can also successfully challenge the explanatory power of DSGE models when confined to their same ground.

3.9.4 Consumption and Buffer Stock

Models built as agent-based computational laboratories offer distinctive opportunities as an experimental tool. In this subsection we provide an illustration of the flexibility of the BAM model by exploring its features as we employ an alternative assumption on households' behavior. Namely, we introduce a variation characterized by individual consumption functions based on simple buffer-stock saving rules (Deaton, 1991; Carroll, 1997), in order to examine in particular their effects on the personal wealth distribution. We will see that in this case the ability of the model to reproduce stylized facts is even improved if compared to the baseline version.

The individual marginal propensity to consume (MPC) c is now derived from an adaptive rule, without any mean-field interaction. In practice, each consumer is supposed to possess a personal desired 'total savings-income' ratio, that she strives to keep constant along her lifetime:

$$\frac{S_{t+1}}{W_t} = h \tag{3.17}$$

where S and W represent total savings and income, respectively. If income at time t increases (decreases), consumers will try to increase (decrease) their savings at time $t+1$ as well. Thus, the actual MPC can change from time to time since it depends on the current income growth rate.

Two alternative spending rules have been tested in simulations. In the first one, consumption depends upon current income only, that is $C_t = c_t W_t$. In the alternative version, consumption is financed drawing on both income and savings, $C_t = c_t(W_t + S_t)$. Interestingly enough, we found that the two rules yield identical long-run results and, consequently, we decided to present here only results obtained by means of the simplest $C_t = c_t W_t$ consumption rule.

We define the desired stock of future savings at time t+1 as past savings plus retained income at time t:

$$S_{t+1} = S_t + (1-c)W_t \tag{3.18}$$

where c is the individual MPC. Plugging (3.18) into (3.17), and defining $W_t = W_{t-1}(1+g_t)$ where g_t is the income growth rate at time t, we get:

$$\frac{S_t}{W_{t-1}(1+g_t)} + (1-c) = h\,. \tag{3.19}$$

If we define $S_t/W_{t-1} = h + d_t$, where d_t is the time t divergence between desired and actual savings-income ratios, we finally obtain the expression for the time t MPC for a generic household:

$$c_t = 1 + \frac{d_t - hg_t}{1+g_t}\,. \tag{3.20}$$

Consumption is then simply defined as $C_t = c_t W_t$.

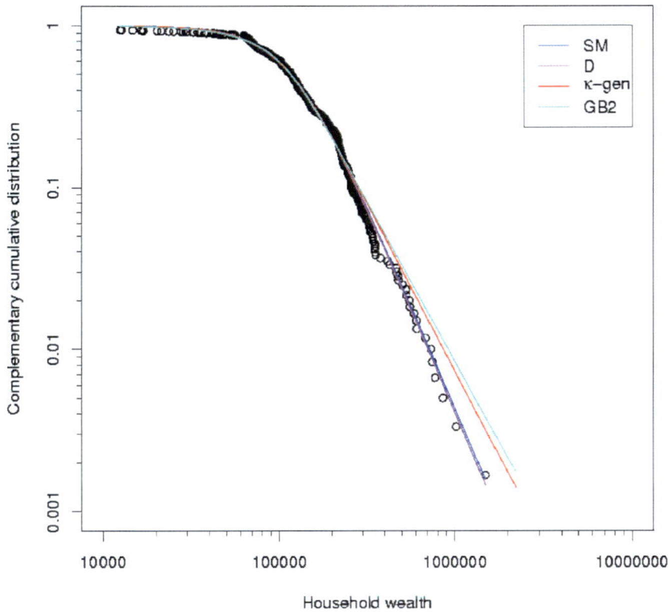

Fig. 3.9 Fitting of the complementary CDF of personal incomes in correspondence of the last simulation period

Once the buffer-stock based consumption rule is employed, the BAM model keeps its ability to return all the basic emergent macroeconomic features shown in Figs. 3.4, 3.5 and 3.6. Furthermore, we discover that its degree of realism is even improved once the personal wealth distribution is considered. In fact, a huge body of recent theoretical and empirical work (Kleiber and Kotz, 2003) has persuasively shown that three statistical functional forms can be considered as the best-fitting candidates to model real data on personal incomes and wealth: *i*) the four-parameter Generalized Beta II (GB2) distribution; *ii*) the Dagum (D) distribution; and *iii*) the Singh-Maddala (SM) distribution. Thus, a natural way to further assess the ability of the modified BAM model to replicate reality consists in applying these three statistical models to cross-section simulated data for personal income. In addition, we test also the κ-Generalized distribution recently introduced by Kaniadakis (2001), and successfully employed in the analysis of income distribution estimation by Clementi *et al.* (2007, 2008).[48] Results from such a distribution fitting exercise can be observed in Fig. 3.9. All the statistical models appear to match remarkably well the simulated data, especially the D and the SM distributions. Even though at this stage we are not even trying to confront punctual esti-

[48] GB2, D and SM can be derived as the solution of a differential-equation Pearson system, with D and SM being three-parameter specializations of the GB2 distribution. The κ-Generalized distribution, on its part, is obtained from the entropy constrained maximization of a deformed exponential function.

mates obtained from real data with estimates for simulated data, from a qualitative point of view this last result confirms once again the amazing ability of the BAM model to generate macroeconomic stylized facts.

3.10 Robustness

In this last section we present some computational tests aimed at checking the robustness of simulation results to changes in the random seeds and in the values of some key parameters (Subsect. 3.10.1). Finally, we explore how our findings are affected by variations of two crucial aspects: the consumers' preference attachment mechanism and the entry mechanism (Subsect. 3.10.2).

3.10.1 Exploration of the Parameter Space

In a typical agent-based model an exhaustive robustness check – a procedure also known as *model verification*, aimed at: *i*) confirming the central results of the simulated model and/or revealing possible output variations when the input parameters are changed; *ii*) guiding future work by drawing attention to the most promising directions for further research – should be performed along the whole grid of parameters and random number seeds through extensive Montecarlo simulations (Fagiolo *et al.*, 2007). According to an increasing consensus among practitioners, for each vector in the parameter space a high number of independent simulations should be run, each one for a different seed of the random number generator. Then, after calculating all the relevant statistics of the simulated data, one should compute their mean and variance across simulations. If the latter is sufficiently small, one can state that the model is stable, and each simulation can be interpreted as representative of the underlying data generating process (DGP). Clearly, such a procedure is extremely demanding. For instance, suppose that in a model there are just 10 relevant parameters, and that each parameter can assume 10 different values (a rather simplifying assumption). As a result, one obtains that the constellation of the parameter space is given by 10^{10} vectors. If we perform 20 different runs for each one of them to take into account the possible effects of changing the random seeds, the total number of simulations would amount to $2*10^{11}$!

Our strategy for robustness checking is far more modest, as we employ the two different techniques involved in a proper model verification procedure, namely *internal validity* and *sensitivity analysis*, in two separate steps. In a first exercise we run a certain number of independent simulations, each one with a different random seed, using the particular parameter vector shown in Table 3.1. If the random seeds employed for the random number generator do not cause large variability of the outcome sample points, the model can be deemed as sufficiently accurate. Second, we choose a selected subset of parameters, and we run several simulations to quantify how changes in the values of the input parameters alter the output. The model is then believed to be *good* if the output values of interest do not vary significantly despite significant changes in the input values.

The aggregate behavior emerging from an averaging of outcomes over 20 alternative random-seed simulations show that the results we have discussed so far are significantly robust. The key qualitative time-series features of growth and cyclical fluctuations remain unaffected, and the cross-simulation variance calculated for typical macroeconomic variables (GDP, productivity, inflation, real wage, unemployment, interest rates, bankruptcy rates) is remarkably small. The distribution of the firms' size (both in terms of sales and net worth) calculated in correspondence of the last simulation period is definitely invariant in its significant departure from normality and its strong positive skewness. Finally, a Phillips curve, an Okun law and a Beveridge curve continue to emerge from each simulation and on average.

Fig. 3.10 reports the structure of co-movements at four leads and lags, plus the contemporaneous one, between the de-trended values of the GDP and of the other five variables already considered in Fig. 3.8. It largely corroborates our previous findings regarding the procyclicality of unemployment, productivity and the real wage, as well as the substantial a-ciclicality of the aggregate price index and of the real interest rate. Furthermore, the signs of the configuration of non-contemporaneous correlation coefficients already found for the baseline simulation is largely confirmed as we control for the stochastic dimension of the model. A final remark is in order to highlight the simulation outcome that proves to be most challenging, namely the auto-regressive structure of the de-trended output and its relative hump-shaped impulse-response pattern. At odds with the result shown in Panel (*f*) of Fig. 3.8, when we consider an average over cross-section simulations, the movement in the log of detrended GPD can be best approximated by an AR(1) structure (with an autoregressive parameter around 0.8). Of course, this calls for further investigations to assess when and how endogenous aggregate positive feedback loops operates in this world.

As regards the second step, we choose to perform a univariate sensitivity analysis, according to which the model outcomes are analyzed with respect to the variation of one parameter at a time, whereas all the other parameters of the system remain constant. For each parameter we run at least four alternative scenarios, with values chosen on rather coarse grids. To somehow summarize our main findings, the parameters that prove to be crucial – in that alternative parameter values change simulation results significantly – are the ones related to the duration of labour contracts, to the number of opportunities any unit is allowed to locally explore as it searches for market transactions (*local* markets), and to the total size of the economy. Let us see them in more detail.

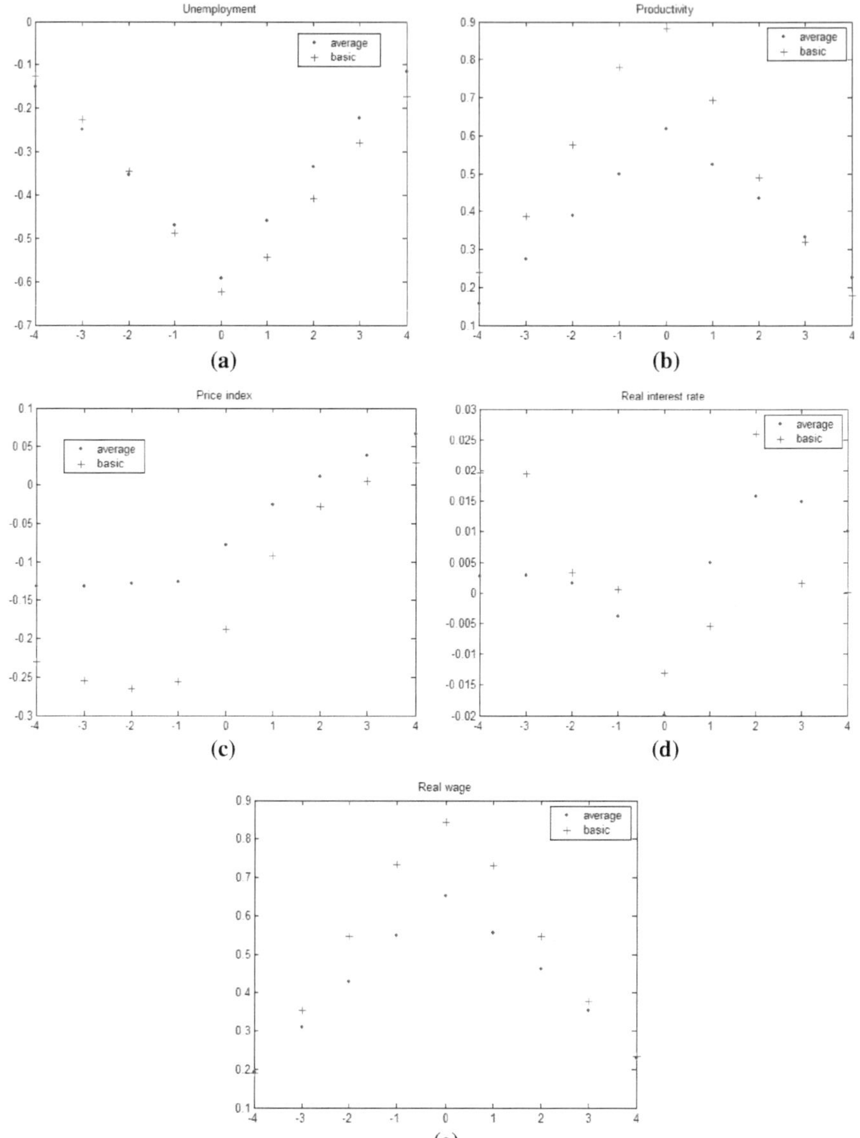

Fig. 3.10 Baseline (+) and cross-simulation mean (°) co-movements at four leads and lags. (**a**) Unemployment; (**b**) productivity; (**c**) price index; (**d**) interest rate; (**e**) real wage

Local credit markets. As we increase the number of banks each firm can borrow from – in particular, as we raise the parameter H from its baseline value from 2 to 3, 4, and 6 – the general properties of the model (in terms of output, productivity, unemployment, inflation, real wages, bankruptcy rates, and so on) do not manifest any significant variation. It must be noted, however, that an increase in H forces the cyclical component of the price index to be coincident with the aggregate output, while the right tail of the size distribution of firms' net worth becomes more and more similar to a Pareto distribution. As the number of potential partners on the credit market is reduced to 1, on the contrary, the size distribution looks more similar to an exponential. A plausible explanation for this feature is as follows. When search costs in the credit market are lower, and accordingly the number of different banks a firm can visit is higher, the probability that firm has to be rationed is relatively smaller, all other things being equal. In terms of the whole population, therefore, firms can fully exploit their proportional growth potential (autocatalicity), and the right tail of the firms' size distribution assumes a Pareto-like behavior.

Local consumption goods markets. The second experiment consists in increasing the number of firms which consumers can visit before purchasing (Z). As we increase Z from 2 to 3, 4, 5 and 6, competition among firms increases, and the function exerted on firms' growth by the preferential attachment mechanism becomes less and less effective. In particular, the real wages become lagging, their co-movement with output similar to those of the price index and, as it is logical, the kurtosis of the firm's size distribution decreases dramatically. Moreover, production displays smoother patterns, without sudden booms or crashes. This happens because in a more competitive environment truly big firms cannot emerge, and consequently systemic risk is more evenly spread across producers.

Local labour markets. The functioning of the labour market is regulated by two crucial parameters: the number of workers' applications (M) and the labour contract length. As far as the former is concerned, we start our sensitivity experiment by decreasing the number of allowable applications from 4 to 3 and 2, discovering that prices switch from being anti-cyclical and leading to pro-cyclical and lagging. Aggregate output shows an higher degree of instability, since firms have a lower probability to fill in their vacancies – and thus to produce planned output – while the upper tail of firms' size distribution appears to become more Pareto-like. Strong path-dependency in the labour market allows the formation of "advantaged" (with a higher probability to fill in their vacancies), and thus more performing, firms. This interpretation is indirectly confirmed as we *increase* the number of applications (to 5 and 6): tougher competition on the labour market and a higher probability to find workers make firms all alike, and their size distribution scales much more as an exponential, or even a uniform. In addition, as one can expect, competition between firms in hiring workers tends to push the real wage up, sometime even above average productivity.

Employment contracts duration. Another relevant parameter tuning the functioning of the labour market is the duration of the employment contracts signed by firms and workers, which in the baseline simulation we set to 8 periods. In order to control for both a very flexible and a quite rigid labour market, we have first decreased it to 6, 4 and 1, to subsequently increase it to 10, 12 and 14. Since we interpret each simulation period as a quarter, the sensitivity experiment thus covers contract durations stemming from one quarter to three years and half. While for intermediate values of the parameter the main statistical properties of the model do not change significantly, the opposite is true for the extreme values, which produce degenerate dynamics. More precisely, decreasing the labour contract length produces a continuous process of creation and dissolution of the network linking workers and employers. This ever-changing network reduces path-dependence, causing co-movements to become less and less pronounced, except for the unemployment rate and real wages, that basically keep on showing the same properties of the baseline simulation. With a contract length of 6 and 4 periods, output becomes smoother and its cyclical component definitely looses the AR(2) structure. Moreover, because of the lessening of path-dependence the bulk of operating firms tends to distribute more uniformly. It is worth noting that, in spite of a more flexible labour market, on the average unemployment increases and output decreases, revealing the presence of coordination failures on a grand scale due to aggregate demand spillovers. In fact, during downturns firms can easily fire workers; consequently, the economy experiences a sensible reduction of the aggregate demand that causes firms to further revise downwards their production plans and labour demand for the subsequent simulation iterations. On the contrary, if firms are forced by longer contracts to hoard labour and to pay wages also during recessions, aggregate demand reduces less, thus preventing the triggering of a vicious circle. The actual functioning of this mechanism is further confirmed by pushing it to the extreme: when labour contracts last only one period, that is when firms are given full freedom of firing, the number of bankruptcies and the unemployment rate reach very high values, and in most of the simulations the whole economy collapses, signaling the presence of fatal market failures.

A different reasoning applies when the labour market is rigid (in our case when the contract duration is equal to 12 periods, or higher). In this case, simulated co-movements contrast sharply with the ones calculated for real data, and time series dynamics are often degenerated. The supply side of the model is now the weakest ring of the chain: because of long contractual commitments, firms cannot resort to firing when they are financially fragile and go bankruptcy more easily. This leads to an overall macroeconomic breakdown.

The size and the structure of the economy. A last sensitivity experiment concerns the role played on simulation outcomes by the absolute size of the economy and its composition. In our context, this amounts to vary the total number of agents populating the economy on the one hand, and the relative frequency of classes (firms, households, banks) over the whole on the other one. In order to shed light upon these issues, we first run small groups of simulations multiplying sequentially the number of all agents by 2, 5 and 10 *without* changing the proportions among the three classes of economic units. As the size of the economy is scaled up, the average growth rate and the statistical properties expressed in terms of co-movements are very similar to their counterparts calculated for the baseline simulation, whereas the time series of macroeconomic variables display rather smoother cyclical fluctuations. The negative relationship between aggregate volatility and the economy's mass we find in simulations can be rationalized intuitively – since macroeconomic volatility tends to reduce as microeconomic specific volatility is averaged out over an increasing number agents – and it is also consistent with a large number of empirical studies based on cross-section international data finding a significant negative relationship between the GDP's variance and the country's size (Barro, 1991; Head, 1995, Canning *et al.*, 1998).

As a second step, we proceed to vary the structural composition of the economy by muting the relative frequencies of the classes of agents operating in this world. In particular, we run three groups of simulations doubling the size of just one class per time, while the size of the other two classes are kept fixed to their baseline values. Interestingly enough, the three experiments lead to different outcomes. Doubling the number of banks does not exert any significant variation to the model's outcomes. When the number of households is increased, in turn, the leads-and-lags co-movement analysis shows a scenario quite similar to that of the baseline simulation, but time series appear to grow much faster – and with a higher volatility – thanks to the enlarged availability of workforce. Conversely, an increase of the proportion of firms has the effect of slowing down the average rate of growth of the economy. This happens because of an increased competition on the credit market (with more rationings occurring), on the labour market (with more unfilled vacancies) and especially on the supply side of the consumption goods market (with lower prices, revenues and profits). Since R&D investments conducing to productivity enhancements are financed out of retained profits, in this world a fiercer competition eventually tends to reduce growth opportunities.

3.10.2 Preferential Attachment in Consumption and the Entry Mechanism

The last part of this section is devoted to an inspection of the influence exerted on the model's output by two mechanisms, one regulating the choice of the preferred supplier exerted by consumers, and the other one regulating the entry process of new firms as bankrupt firms leave the market.

Recall that in the baseline BAM model discussed above, consumers are allowed to search for a satisficing deal inside a local market composed of Z firms. At each time period, Z-1 of them are chosen randomly, while the last one is in any case the largest (in terms of its scale of production) firm visited during the previous round. This mechanism corresponds to a localized preferential attachment (PA) scheme, and in our context it plays a double role. From the point of view of consumers, maintaining the largest firm they have knowledge of inside their search space allow them to minimize the risk of being rationed, *ceteris paribus*. Since it is not directly influenced by pricing concerns, the common preference for larger firms creates a type of non-market – or *social* – interaction among consumers: the higher the number of people who have previously chosen a certain firm, the higher the probability that I choose that firm as well. The localized PA scheme, in turn, provides a structure to the topology of the market interactions' network linking firms and consumers. In particular, it endows the economy with a high degree of granularity, with the largest firms becoming even larger as they take advantage of the loyalty of customers and grow to a size not attainable under a pure random network.

To control for the influence exerted by the localized PA scheme on the structure of business fluctuations, we run 20 independent simulations of a pure-random-network version of the BAM model, holding all else constant. The experiment tells us that in the absence of the localized PA mechanism there is a sensible gain in stability, in that the volatility of all relevant macroeconomic variables decrease steadily. As a matter of example, the time series for the GDP obtained from a representative simulation is shown in Fig. 3.11: growth is still fluctuating, but deep crisis disappear completely. The reason why this happens is intuitive: the PA mechanism increases the path-dependence of choices and, at the same time, it makes the economy's volatility greater since it allows the formation of very large firms, whose behavior deeply affects the entire system for the reasons we have explored before. Thus, we can argue that the topology of the networks structuring an economic system plays an important role in its functioning and performance: social interaction *matters* and cannot be ignored without consequences. Furthermore, the localized PA scheme can be suitably tuned to calibrate our agent-based model by means of real data on macroeconomic volatility.

The new co-movement structure resembles its counterparts of the baseline simulation, with the exception of the price index and of real wages that now become lagging, even if for any practical purpose they can still be deemed as a-cyclical. The autoregressive structure of output's cyclical component turns firmly

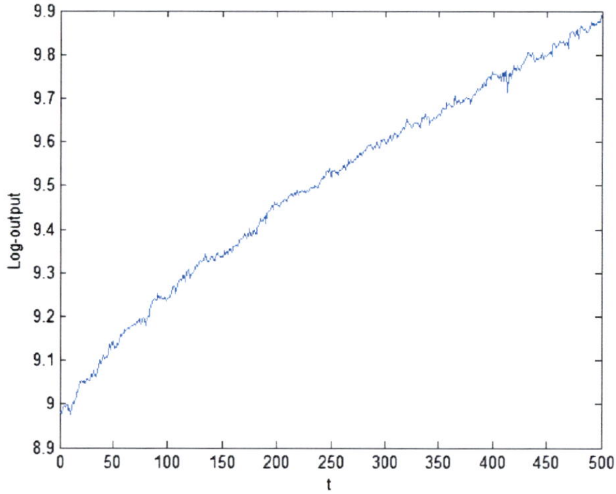

Fig. 3.11 Log of GDP for a representative simulation without the preferential attachment in consumption mechanism

into an AR(1) process with an auto-regressive coefficient around 0.4, while the firms' size distribution becomes significantly less skew. Hence, moving from a PA scheme to a fully random network linking consumers and sellers produces results that are similar to those obtained previously when we lowered transaction costs on local consumption goods markets. As we perform small clusters of simulations for different points in the parameter space, we discover that the model's outcome preserves all its key features. In particular, this holds true when the sizes of local markets agents can visit each time period are either increased and decreased (that is, when searching costs are varied).

Finally, we turn to evaluate the consequences produced by the firms' entry-exit mechanism on the model's outcomes. In Subsect. 3.9.2 we provided an explanation of emergent output fluctuations based on the endogenous dynamics of financial fragility. However, one could wonder whether business cycle dynamics (i.e., the recurrence of booms, busts and recoveries) actually depends just on endogenous mechanisms, or if it relies also upon the exogenous and automatic introduction in the system of new well capitalized firms whenever bankrupt firms exit. Consequently, in order to explore this issue we run a modified version of the model where firms' profits are heavily taxed by an unmodeled internal revenues office, but revenues are not redistributed into the system. This trick is basically intended to increase the firms' financial fragility, thus producing a higher probability of insolvency. If the automatic entry process is really distortional, the model should display a somehow better performance as the number of bankrupt firms is increased. In spite of the higher systemic financial fragility, in fact, the massive entrance of new financially-sound firms should counterbalance the negative effects caused by the transfer of firms from a speculative to a Ponzi position. Actually, in correspondence of a higher average number of bankruptcies the overall economic behavior shows a substantially worse performance, both in terms of lower growth and of higher volatility. Hence, we argue that the automatic entry mechanism is likely to be neutral, confirming the endogenous explanation of economic dynamics.

Chapter 4
Empirical Validation

> No one who has experienced the intense involvement of computer modeling would deny that the temptation exists to use any data input that will enable one to continue playing what is perhaps the ultimate game of solitaire.
>
> JAMES LOVELOCK
> *Gaia: A New Look at Life on Earth*, pp. 129

4.1 The Empirics of Falsificationism

The aim of this chapter is to understand to what extent the BAM model described and simulated in Chap. 3 is able to reproduce real world phenomena, by applying tools and techniques of *empirical external validation* (see Fagiolo *et al.*, 2007).

As argued at length before, our framework allows us to explore the macroeconomic outcomes generated by the market and non-market interactions of a large population of heterogeneous agents. Starting from simple behavioural rules at the individual level, some aggregate statistical regularities emerge that could not be inferred from the behaviour of single agents in isolation. This *emergent* behaviour often feeds back on individuals, affecting their actions in turn. In other words, micro and macroeconomic behaviours co-evolve in an adaptive way. From this viewpoint, the pattern of the aggregate is not the result of a simple summation and averaging of individual preferences and choices, but it is the product of self-organization "from the bottom-up". A self-organized macroeconomy is furthermore susceptible of abrupt phase transitions when a scenario of criticality occurs.

So far, we have presented simulations carried out using ad hoc parameters' values and the same initial set up for all the agents belonging to the same class. To paraphrase Nicholas Kaldor, we have just started from some hypothesis that could account for some stylized facts (say, the tendency of modern economies to fluctuate around a growing path), without necessarily adhere to historical accuracy (Kaldor, 1965). Using an initial set up of actual Italian data, we currently aim at verifying whether the BAM model, simulated over a period for which actual data are fully available, is an acceptable representation of the actual system at micro, meso and macroeconomic scales. In a nutshell, we intend to perform an *ex-post validation* of a microsimulated version of the model. We shall be in a position to conclude that the result of this validation exercise is positive if the model outcome represents a good approximation of the actual data generating process. While the validation process should not be regarded in any case as a formal prerequisite for the development of an ABC model and for a discussion of its predictions (Carley, 1996), a careful assessment of the adequacy and accuracy of the model in matching real world data should help us in resisting the temptation referred to in the epigraph to this chapter.

As we will see, the BAM model is able to reproduce the dynamics of actual data with a good degree of precision along several dimensions. In particular, it nicely replicates some interesting cross-sectional results about size distributions and other remarkable pieces of empirical evidence.

4.2 On the Microfoundation of Agent-based Models

By common wisdom, ABC models possess micro-foundations almost by definition, given that the assumed behaviour of artificial agents is always based on specific micro-rules. Moreover, this kind of models are generally considered satisfactory if and only if they are to some extent able to reproduce aggregate empirical evidence and statistical regularities. However, such a position must be somehow qualified, since ABC models are not naturally and necessarily micro-founded. The right question to be posed is in fact empirical in nature: are we sure that the micro-rules driving the dynamics of the disperse system are really based on empirical evidence and actual data? The answer one can give is essential to decide whether an agent-based model can be validated or not, especially in its microsimulated version when the model itself is initialized and continuously compared with actual data.

According to this approach, a really micro-founded ABC model should be based on the following prerequisites:

- the agents' initial conditions should be initialized with actual data;
- the behavioural rules, structural equations and all the other elements governing the evolution of the system should be based, whenever possible, on statistics-based data analysis. If direct data analysis is not possible, updating rules should rely on surveys' results or on experimental evidence;
- researchers should specify the physical meaning they attach to simulation times. Does a simulation period correspond to one year, to one quarter, or to one day?

Let us see in more detail the practical implications stemming from these three requirements.

If the original endowments and the other starting conditions of artificial agents are initialized with actual data, one of the major criticisms levelled to ABC models (especially for their use as policy tools) – that is, the initial homogeneity (apart from random dislocations) of the agents belonging to the same class – can be easily avoided. While in many cases it is interesting to study the emergence of heterogeneity from homogeneous initial conditions *per se*, it is also true that during a simulation run it is rather difficult to isolate from initial transitional phases the portion in which the system can actually reproduce the desired microeconomic *and* macroeconomic phenomena. By the same token, the initial running-in periods are particularly critical when performing sensitivity analysis, since micro state variables are generally unstable, so that it is not easy to understand their marginal impact in the model.

Similar issues hold as we regards agents' behavioural rules. In many ABC models, microeconomic rules of conduct are so discretional and based on stochastic disturbances that it is practically impossible to discern their impact on the whole system, apart from very trivial cases. Moreover, if behavioural rules are not based on data observations, it remains unclear how could an ABC model be possibly considered as a policy-oriented tool.

Finally, any modelling choice on the physical meaning one must assign to simulation time periods is strictly related to the preceding points. If a model is initialized with actual data and micro-founded rules, comparisons of simulation results and actual data are much easier, and the physical meaning to be attached to simulation times can be defined naturally. For example, if we consider yearly actual data and we discover that a distance metric between them and simulations results is minimized on the average every two simulation periods, then we can assert that each simulation period corresponds to a semester. If, on the contrary, such a distance is minimized in every single period then one simulation time is equal to one actual year. It goes without saying that a correct understanding of the physical meaning of simulation time is also essential for policy purposes.

These practical issues are at the heart of a methodological distinction between two general categories of ABC models: *i*) *pure* ABC models, which must not necessarily be taken to the data to preserve their theoretical relevance as soon as microspecifications are plausible, and that are mainly useful to explain through generative techniques the mechanics of emergent aggregate phenomena under different rules of behaviour; *ii*) *applied* ABC models, which are conceived from the start in a form which admits microsimulation. While pure agent-based models, apart from some heuristical observations regarding emerging statistical regularities and evidences, are not externally validable almost by definition, applied ABC models need and have to be descriptively validated (i.e., compared with actual data) and calibrated (i.e., all the parameters' values must be chosen with the aim of better approximating reality). Only microsimulated ABC models can be effectively validated in a complete statistical sense, either *ex-ante* (in terms of the microfoundation on data and empirical evidence of behavioural rules), *ex-post* (in terms of a comparison over time between simulations' outcomes and actual data), and *simultaneously* (by the means of parameter calibration).

In order to accomplish this task, both the availability and the quality of micro-economic data is essential. As we shall discuss in the next lines, the BAM model of Chap. 3 possesses some components for which actual data are not (or not completely) readily available, in particular those referring to the entry and exit processes of firms and to the characteristics of the transactional networks linking agents in the markets for consumption goods and credit.[49] In what follows those parts will be considered in terms of degrees of freedom of the model, and thus not taken into account in our validation experiment. The bulk of the analysis will focus instead on firm-level balance sheet data, industrial dynamics and labour incomes.

4.3 Data Description

The greater part of the validation experiments and of the empirical analysis we present in this chapter are based on firm-level observations from the CEBI database. CEBI, which is probably the most comprehensive Italian dataset collecting balance sheet information on business units, was originally set up by the Bank of Italy, and it is actually maintained by *Centrale dei Bilanci Srl*.[50] In particular, we shall consider annual data, over the period 1988–2002, on a balanced panel of about 25,000 Italian non-financial firms, all satisfying the following requirements:

- reliable data on the level of real productive assets (capital);
- a net worth of at least 20,000 euros;
- at least 5 employees and labour costs of at least 20,000 euros per year.

Reliability of the data at the firm level essentially means that we exclude outliers characterized by unrealistic levels and changes of total assets, defined as the sum of net worth and total liabilities. The thresholds imposed at the level of 20,000 euros of net worth and of 5 employees aims at eliminating from the pool all really small firms, whose behaviour is usually erratic. For each firm and year, we can retrieve from CEBI the following variables from the dataset: firm ID, number of employees, total labour costs, equity, total assets, current liabilities, interest payments, sales, operating turnover, profits and losses, ROI, ROE, and the gearing ratio.

The use in our validation experiment of a balanced panel comes with both strengths and weaknesses. On the one hand, it assures continuity in the data, thus simplifying the analysis and allowing for clear-cut conclusions. On the other hand, it rules out by construction entry-exit processes. This is a significant limitation, since bankruptcy plays a crucial role in the BAM model. A possible way out of this problem could be the use of a complementary dataset composed of a subset of firms, from which to pick a substitute every time a firm exits from the panel. Even

[49] This does not mean that these data could not be collected in principle. Think for instance to the mass of proprietary data which could be easily retrieved (… if priced at their marginal costs) from the electronic records registering the transactions executed in large chain-stores by possessors of fidelity cards.

[50] See the *Centrale dei Bilanci* website at http://www.centraledeibilanci.it.

abstracting from the obvious critique that these substituting firms would not represent new entries in a proper sense, this solution would create even bigger problems concerning the "representativeness" of the firms' size distribution and its stability. For all these reasons, we decide to stick to the simpler "balanced" approach.

To complete the information about the labour market, we shall also use the so-called WHIP (Work Histories Italian Panel) database, developed by the Laboratorio Revelli of the University of Turin.[51] WHIP is a database of individual work histories, based on administrative archives at INPS (the Italian Social Security Institute), in which the main episodes of the working career of each individual in the sample are observed and recorded. The reference population is made up by all the people (both Italian and foreign citizens) who have worked in Italy even only for part of their career. The complete list of available observations includes: private employee working contracts; atypical contracts; self-employment activities as artisan, trader and some activities as freelancer; retirement spells and unemployment spells during which the individual received social benefits, like unemployment subsidies or mobility benefits. The sample is really large and representative of the total population of employees in the private sector. Workers in the public sector and professionals (lawyers, engineers, etc.) – who are covered by a social security provider different from INPS – are not recorded in WHIP, however.

4.4 Validation Procedure

The validation procedure we propose in this context is a mix of established statistical techniques and other innovative methods only recently applied in this area (see Bianchi *et al.*, 2007, 2008), and it is largely based on well-known results developed in the fields of computational models' evaluation (Kleijnen, 1995) and extreme value theory (Embrechts *et al.*, 1997). In particular, the iterative validation procedure followed below is made up of three steps:

1. a microsimulation of the model using actual data to calibrate it;
2. a descriptive validation of the simulated output;
3. if the output validation is satisfactory, then stop; otherwise re-calibrate the model and re-start from point 1.

Microsimulation is a technique operating at the level of individual units, like households or firms, that are always required to be initialized with actual data. Within the model, each unit is represented by a record containing a unique identifier and a set of associated attributes. A collection of rules are then applied to these units, leading to simulated changes in states and behaviours. Rules may change according to deterministic drivers, such as changes in tax liabilities resulting from changes in tax regulations, or because of stochastic variations. In both cases, as a result of applying these empirically based rules of action over many

[51] The dataste is available at http://www.laboratoriorevelli.it under the WHIP section.

time steps one gets numerical values for the state variables characterizing each unit, as well as for the distributional features of any change.

Bianchi *et al.* (2007) have proposed the use of microsimulation techniques as a means for validating agent-based models. The idea is rather simple: if an agent-based model is meant to reproduce empirical evidence to some extent, once it is initialized with actual data it should be able to reproduce real world phenomena with a certain level of precision. In other words, the model is first set up with the available actual data. Then it is simulated without any further intervention. Finally, simulated and actual data are compared at the end of the simulation and for each intermediate time period. From this point of view, any ABC model is well validated if its microsimulated version can sufficiently approximate reality. The higher the ability of the model in fitting real-world data, the more the model is judged as reliable. The microsimulated agent-based model can then be the starting point of a calibration exercise, meant to reduce the distance between actual and simulated data. Different techniques are available for these purposes. A good example is represented by indirect inference, as shown in Bianchi *et al.* (2007) and Gilli and Winker (2003).

There are also several graphical and statistical tools available either to perform a descriptive analysis of results, as well as to compare actual and simulated data in order to determine to what extent the microsimulated model reproduces observed data. First of all, the main characteristics of the data can be assessed by means of simple distributional fitting exercises (histograms, smoothed density plots, Zipf's plots, box-plots). Second, a comparison between simulated and actual data can be based both on graphical tools (quantile-quantile [Q-Q] plots, probability-probability [P-P] plots, mean excess function versus threshold [MEPLOT] plots), and on related tests aimed at weighing against the basic descriptive statistics and position means of the two data sets (Kruskal-Wallis tests and empty box tests). Finally, the corresponding distributions can be further analyzed and compared using formal goodness-of-fit tests, like the Kolmogorov-Smirnov (based on the supremum metric), the Cramér-Von Mises (which makes use of a quadratic measure of distance), and the Anderson-Darling (very powerful but not distribution-free, since critical values depend on the distribution under scrutiny). In the next sections we shall show how these tools and techniques can be used to assess the validity of the BAM model.

4.5 Firms' Size and Growth

A profusion of empirical investigations in industrial dynamics have detected two cross-sectional empirical regularities, which are amazingly widespread across countries and persistent over time:

1. The distribution of firms' size (measured in terms of total assets, sales and employment) is in general right skewed, and it can often be well described by a power law probability density function (Axtell, 2000; 2001; Gaffeo *et al.*, 2003; Okuyama *et al.*, 1999; Quandt, 1966; Ramsden and Kiss-Haypal, 2000; Simon, 1955).

2. Firms' growth rates are Laplace distributed, a model which can be nested in the larger and more flexible Subbotin's family of distributions (Stanley *et al.*, 1996; Bottazzi and Secchi, 2005).

Delli Gatti *et al.* (2008) have already shown analytically and computationally that facts 1 and 2 (in addition to many other distributional regularities) are at the heart of several financial and business cycle facts. To be considered a model capable of generating a macrostructure of interest, also the BAM model should be able to replicate such an empirical evidence. The first part of the validation exercise is therefore focused on this.

Let us start by considering total assets. Accepting a maximum deviation of ±15% between observed and simulated data, in 2002 (the last year for which we have data) we succeed in reproducing 20888 firms, that is almost 84% of the sample. This is a remarkably good percentage, and similar values can be found in all previous years. Also the distribution obtained by pooling observations over time is correctly fitted for 20391 productive units over a total of 24867 (82%).[52] Fig. 4.1 reports the Zipf's plot of actual and simulated data for the year 2002, showing that the two distributions are almost overlapping. Both observed and simulated capital distributions are particularly skewed, with really fat right tails. Most of the actual firms which are not correctly approximated by their artificial clones are concentrated in the very upper tail, indicating that the model is not fully adequate in reproducing the dynamics of very large companies. This difficulty is likely due to the peculiar structure and dynamics of large firms, whose behaviour is known to be sensibly different from those of other firms (Cirillo and Hüsler, 2009).

In order to assess whether the goodness of fit reported above is due to the adequacy of the model rather than to the characteristics of actual data, we further perform an empirical analysis aimed at verifying how the real firms comprised in our sample changed in size during the time span considered. Indeed, it could be the case that the model does a good job in fitting the real-world system in a given year merely by chance. If the variability of actual data over time is small, therefore, one could erroneously attribute a dynamic similarity between the simulation outcomes and the data to the model's generative capability. On the contrary, if the actual data vary a lot over time and – in spite of this – the BAM model does a god job in fitting them, the confidence we can pose on its adequacy is necessarily higher.

In Fig. 4.2 one can perform a comparison, by means of Zipf's plots, among the cross-sectional distributions of actual balance sheet data on total assets in 1988, 1995 and 2002. The inference from simple visual inspection is quite clear: there is a substantial difference between the three sets of data. If we accept the usual ±15% confidence interval, less than 17% of the firms (essentially the ones that have changed a little over time) can be considered as contemporaneously fitting the data in all samples. In fact, even if all distributions seem to belong to

[52] As in Ijiri *et al.* (1977), the use of pooled distributions is possible since the yearly distributions show similar slopes.

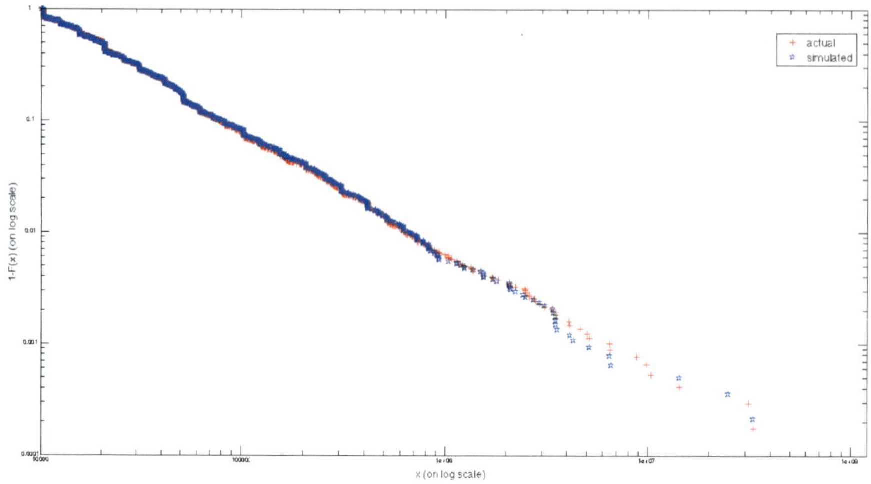

Fig. 4.1 Zipf's plot of total assets distributions: actual and simulated in year 2002

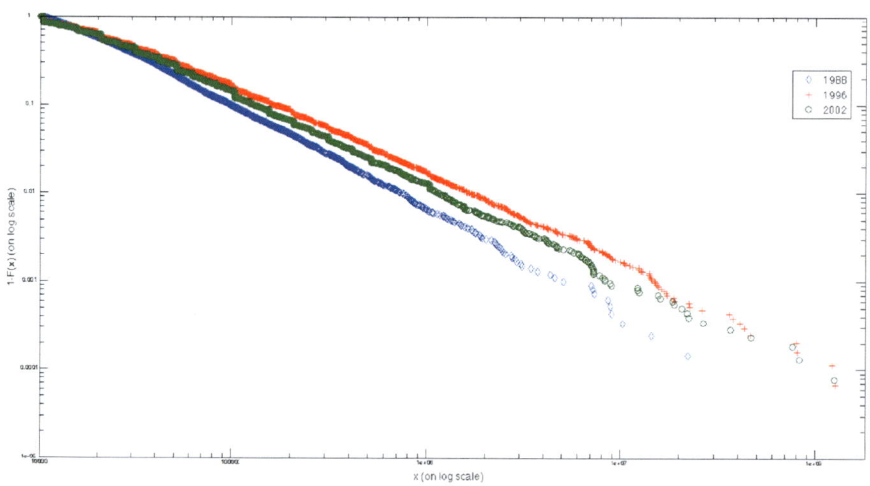

Fig. 4.2 Evolution of actual total assets in years 1998, 1995 and 2002

the same family, their shape and scale parameters are sensibly different. Several additional analytical tools, such as the Kolmogorov-Smirnov's statistics and the Anderson-Darling's test for power laws, confirm this result.

Another informative test can be easily built by calculating the average growth rate of actual firms between 1988 and 2002, to subsequently let the artificial firms – calibrated with actual balance sheet data for the starting year 1988 – grow at this factor in each subsequent simulation period. If the actual growth process is trivially linear, this experiment should allow artificial firms to reproduce actual data in 2002 with an acceptable level of precision. However, the result obtained in this way is rather poor: only 44% of the sample in 2002 is correctly fitted, against a percentage of 84% of the BAM model.

Once the issue of whether the BAM model is able to generate macroscopic regularities of interest from empirically-based microspecifications has been positively addressed, we are in a good position to further assess the degree of matching between the model and the real data. To do this, we make use of several graphical and analytical tests aimed at checking if the observed and simulated samples can be considered belonging to the same distribution. For instance, as shown in Fig. 4.3 a Q-Q plot computed for the year 2002 clearly supports the hypothesis that both samples are drawn from the same statistical distribution. Similar findings – not shown here to save space – can be obtained in all the other years. These results can be further corroborated by means of alternative graphical methods (for instance, box-plots), and formal statistical testing procedures (like generalized Kolmogorov-Smirnov [Prabhakar *et al.*, 2003] tests at the 95% confidence level).

As we exclude from the samples – for the reasons reported for instance in Cirillo and Hüsler (2009) – the right upper tails with a cut-off value at the top 12%, both the actual and the simulated data follow a Singh-Maddala distribution. Table 4.1 reports the maximum likelihood point estimates of the relevant parameters for four representative equally spaced years. Similar estimates can be obtained for all the other years not reported here.

The MEPLOT reported in Fig. 4.4 suggests that the right tails of the two distributions display a Paretian behaviour, as signalled by the upward slope of their mean excess function. In order to see whether the two samples possess a similar behaviour, we therefore estimate the shape parameter characterizing their right tails by means of the semiparametric Hill's method.

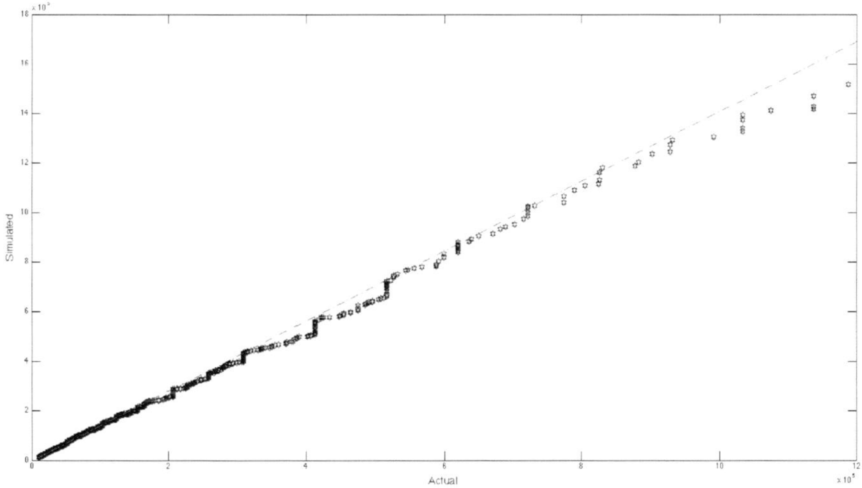

Fig. 4.3 Q-Q plot for actual and simulated total assets in year 2002

Table 4.1 Estimates of the parameters of the Singh-Maddala distribution for actual and simulated data in four different years

Year	*Data*	α	β	γ	ρ
1988	Actual	1.61	93.114	0.96	7.22
	Simulated	1.63	92.737	0.96	7.26
1992	Actual	1.64	97.333	0.98	6.89
	Simulated	1.66	98.122	1.01	6.93
1996	Actual	1.81	99.282	0.93	7.02
	Simulated	1.85	100.071	0.91	7.04
2002	Actual	1.98	101.668	0.99	6.97
	Simulated	1.96	102.002	0.97	6.96

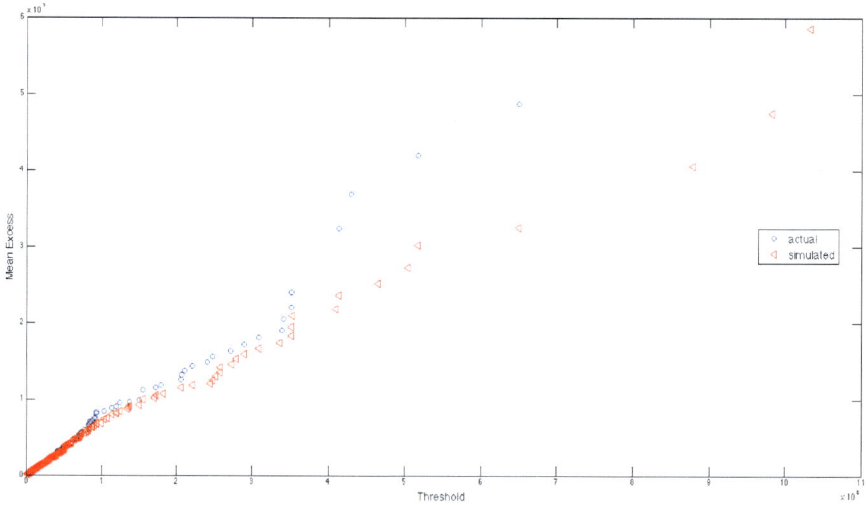

Fig. 4.4 Mean Excess Function plot for actual and simulated total assets

The point estimate we obtain for simulated data is $\alpha=1.81$, while for the actual sample the corresponding value is $\alpha=1.79$. The two parameters are quite similar and belong to the Paretian support ($0.8<\alpha<2$). Notice, however, that the distribution for simulated total assets shows a slightly thinner tail, a finding which further confirms the difficulty of the present version of the BAM model in replicating the behaviour of really large firms, and a pointer for further research.

The following step consists in the empirical validation of the net worth of firms. If we agree to the usual $\pm 15\%$ limit band for deviations between actual and simulated data in 2002, we are able to reproduce the individual histories of 74% of the population. This figure, although largely satisfactory in itself, is somewhat lower than that for total assets. Such a result is likely due to two basic aspects of the BAM model which have been introduced at this stage for the sake of computational tractability: 1) the equity market is not present in the model, and this influences the overall dynamics of firms' balance sheet items, especially of the largest ones; 2) the BAM model lacks enough structure in the formulation of how R&D investments are funded out of retained profits, which are currently modelled in terms of linear relationships.

Apart from these drawbacks which must be fixed in future versions, from a distributional-fitting point of view the BAM model works pretty well also in the case of net worth. As shown by the Zipf's plots reported in Fig. 4.5, the two distributions for the actual and simulated data – calculated in the last period of simulation (2002) – present an unambiguous Paretian behaviour. Hill's estimates of the shape parameters are $\alpha = 1.73$ for actual data, and $\alpha = 1.77$ for simulated data.

The results we get about loans are very similar to those of total assets, since we succeed in fitting about 80% of the firms. Similarly to total assets and net worth, both graphical and analytical tests support the idea of a common density function for both the actual and the simulated debt's data generating processes. It is interesting to notice that, as in Fujiwara (2004), the distribution of loans is in fact a power law. The Hill's estimates of the shape parameters of the Paretian right tails are $\alpha = 1.67$ and $\alpha = 1.64$ for the actual and for the simulated data, respectively, signalling a slight overestimate of the model as regards the largest firms.

The next issue to be explored is the growth dynamics of firms, measured once again in terms of total assets. Several empirical studies have pointed out that the empirical distribution of firms' growth rates is invariably tent-shaped (Hall, 1987; Axtell, 2000). In particular, the best-fitting candidates are the truncated-Lévy model (Gabaix *et al.*, 2003) and the Laplace (or double-exponential) model (Amaral *et al.*, 1997), which has been recently treated as a specialization of the

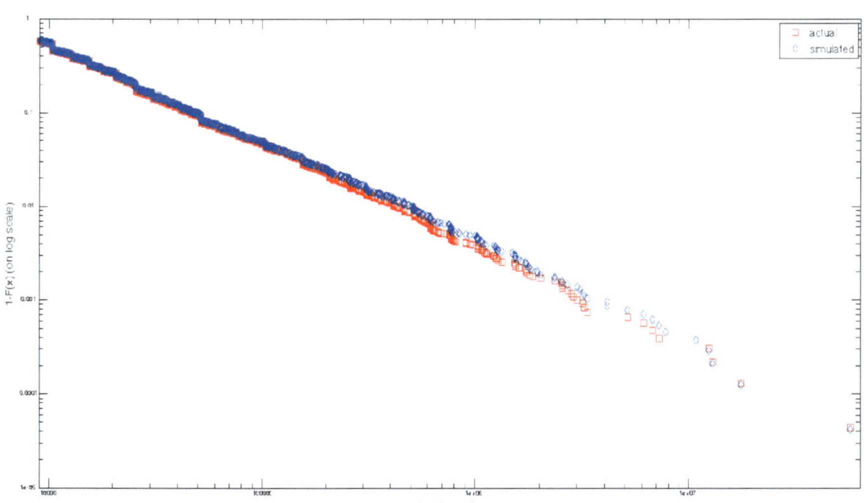

Fig. 4.5 Zipf's plot of net worth distributions: actual and simulated in year 2002

more general Subbotin (Subbotin, 1923) model (Bottazzi and Secchi, 2005). The functional form of Subbotin family of distributions is:

$$f(x,a,b)=\frac{1}{2ab^{\frac{1}{b}}\Gamma\left(1+\frac{1}{b}\right)}e^{-\frac{1}{b}\left|\frac{x-\mu}{a}\right|^{b}} \tag{4.1}$$

where μ is the mean, b and a are two different shape parameters, and Γ is the standard Gamma function. If $b \to 1$, the Subbotin distribution reduces to a Laplace, whereas for $b \to 2$ it approaches a Gaussian. The point estimates for the three Subbotin's parameters – obtained by means of maximum likelihood methods – as we fit this model to our actual and simulated data are reported in Table 4.2.

Table 4.2 Estimates of the Subbotin parameters

	Observed data	*Simulated data*
μ	0.001	0.001
a	0.067	0.061
b	1.006	1.013

At a first glance, the results obtained for observed and simulated growth rates display several similarities. The two means μ are very close to zero, as expected. Since the estimated values of b approach 1 in both cases, the two distributions are in the field of attraction of the Laplace model, excluding normality and, indirectly, ruling away the possibility that a pure Gibrat's law holds true either in reality and in simulations. The values for the Laplacian shape parameter a, finally, are quite similar, even if simulated data show slightly thinner tails. Overall, we can say that the BAM model is able to mimic firms' growth dynamics with a remarkably degree of accuracy. As already noted, the bulk of the problems in the empirical validation of industrial dynamics are concentrated in mimicking the behaviour of firms over the far right tail.

4.6 Interest Rates

Some other interesting results can be obtained by analyzing the functioning of the credit market, focusing in particular on the temporal path followed by interest rates on loans. The graph in Fig. 4.6 allows a visual comparison between the average nominal interest rate obtained in the micro-simulated version of the BAM model and the average interest rate paid by actual firms, as extrapolated from the CEBI database, over the whole time horizon 1988–2002. In particular, we notice that in both cases from 1988 to 1992 the average interest rate paid by firms on their debts has increased, to subsequently decrease steadily. The nearness of the

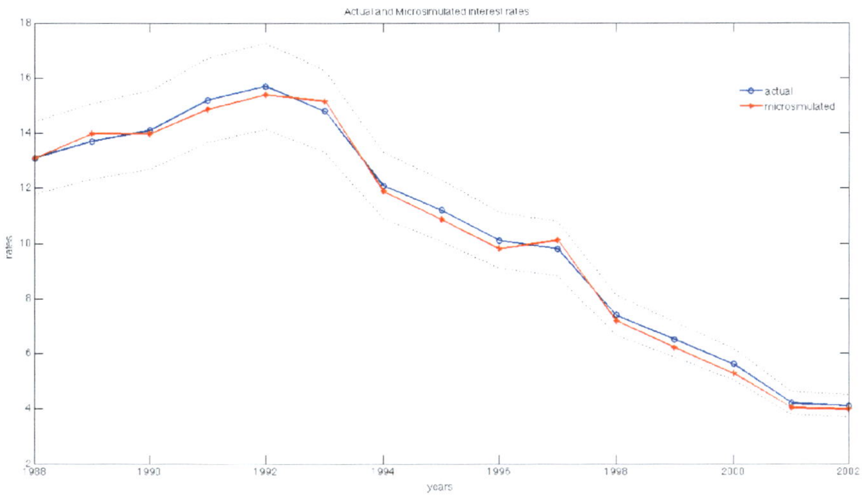

Fig. 4.6 Average interest rate paid on debt: actual and simulated data, 1988–2002

two time series is really remarkable, as the distance between them is always comprised inside a ± 6% deviation range from the mean calculated for the actual data.

In addition to the average rate, in simulations we are also able to track at any time step the interest rate paid to the banking sector by each single firm. If we accept the usual ± 15% deviation from the actual path as a measure of success, the model is able to reproduce the single-firm interest rate dynamics for 57% of the companies comprised in the CEBI dataset, a result we believe to be largely satisfactory given the simplicity of the market microstructure we use in the version of the BAM model discussed so far. Obviously, given the incompleteness of the data at our disposal, we cannot empirically validate other aspects of the model, such as the demand and the supply of loanable funds.

4.7 The Labour Market

The assessment of the labour market is for sure the most difficult part of the whole validation experiment. The ultimate reason is that the data available for the labour market are in general not as accurate and complete as the one for firms' balance sheets we have employed in the previous sections. In particular, the two key problems are that it is rather difficult to obtain accurate microeconomic data for effective wages and other labour-related variables (benefits, hours worked, and so on) on the one hand, and that of it is far from immediate to match these kind of data with the ones on production and credit referred to a particular firm, on the other one.

To partly overcome this difficulty, in this last section we perform an empirical validation of the BAM model's labour market by combining information from the

CEBI and the WHIP databases. As a matter of facts, the WHIP database contains panel-type information about the distributions of Italian wages by firms' dimensions, defined in terms of the number of employees. For all the five dimensional classes available ([0–9], [10–19], [20–199], [20–999] and [1000+]) for every year, a preliminary analysis of the data suggest that the wage distributions are three-modal and can be well approximated by a mixture of three Gaussian distributions, even if better fits – for example by means of Bernstein's polynomials – are obviously available (see Cirillo, 2009). Thanks to the conditions we have previously imposed on the CEBI dataset, we proceed to exclude all firms belonging to the two smallest classes. In other words, in order to guarantee consistency with our previous analysis, we eliminate from the WHIP dataset all firms with less than 20 employees. Fig. 4.7 shows the wage distribution in 1988 for the three dimensional classes remained.

The labour market is then initialized as follows. First, for every firm we sample the wages received by its total work-force from the wage distribution of the dimensional class to which it belongs. Second, for every firm the sampling process is stopped when the total cost of wages is as close as possible to the actual one, as obtained from the CEBI dataset. In particular we accept the standard ±15% difference. This means that for each single firm we may have a small difference between actual and initialized data but, on the average, actual total labour costs are well replicated by the micro-simulated model. If during the simulation a firm hires new workers, their wages are sampled from the corresponding wage distribution as usual.

Because of the lack of suitable data, in this block of micro-simulations the labour market mechanisms of the original BAM model is somehow simplified. In

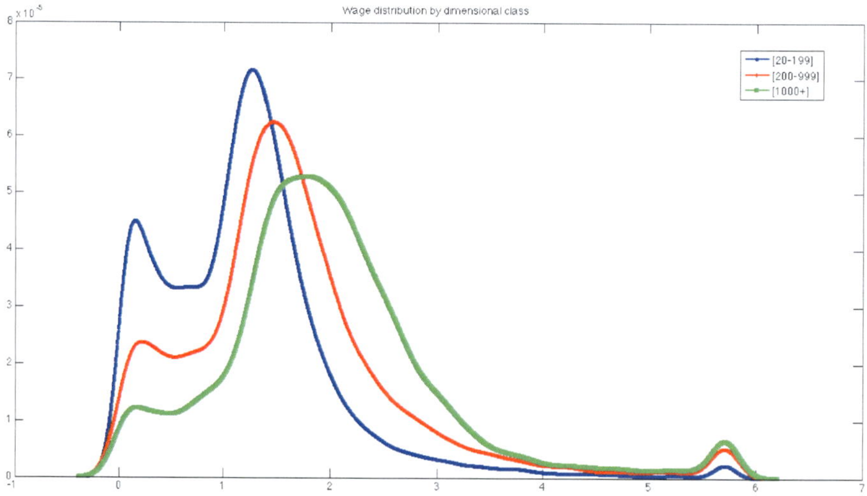

Fig. 4.7 Wage distributions for the classes of dimension [20–199], [20–999] and [1000+] in year 1988

particular, we abstract from the duration of labour contracts, while artificial firms have no particular constraints but the consistency of their total labour costs with those of their actual counterparts. As far as wages are concerned, their growth rate (the quantity ξ_{it} of the model) is set equal to the average actual growth in the WHIP dataset, for the three dimensional classes considered.

As we have seen in the previous sections, our agent-based model is able to reproduce the empirical evidence obtained from actual data with a good degree of precision. Also in the case of the labour market the model seems to be quite accurate, and its weaknesses should be interpreted as useful pointers for further research. In particular, while it is neither possible nor reasonable to look for validating aggregate empirical laws (Beveridge and Okun curves, for example) because of the actual incompleteness of the data, it is interesting to analyze the behaviour of the micro-simulated wage distribution. Specifically, it seems worthy to assess what happens at the end of the simulation, in order to gauge whether the model is able at least to replicate the three-modal feature of actual data. Fig. 4.8 reports the comparisons between the actual and the micro-simulated wage distributions in 2002 for the upper three dimensional classes.

Actual and micro-simulated distributions are quite similar, the scale is consistent, three-modality is present and the distances among the empirical and simulated cumulative density functions are not sufficiently small to pass a Kolmogorov-Smirnov test at the standard 5% significance level, but its statistic is almost borderline at the 10% statistical level. The availability of improved data would have allowed us to better calibrate the model's parameter using simultaneous techniques such as indirect inference or simulated annealing (Gourieroux and Monfort, 1996; Das and Chakrabart, 2005).

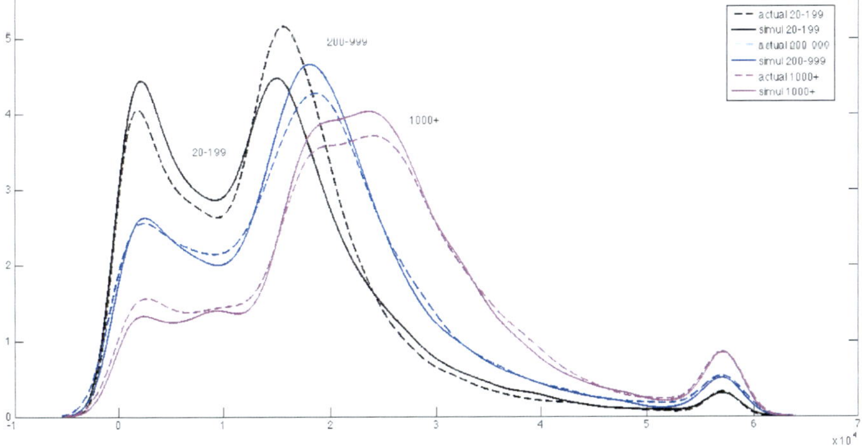

Fig. 4.8 Comparison of wage distributions between actual and simulated data for the classes of dimension [20–199], [20–999] and [1000+] in year 2002

Chapter 5
Conclusions

> Scientific development depends in part on a process of non-incremental or revolutionary change. Some revolutions are large, like those associated with the names of Copernicus, Newton, or Darwin, but most are much smaller, like the discovery of oxygen or the planet Uranus. The usual prelude to changes of this sort is, I believed, the awareness of anomaly, of an occurrence or set of occurrences that does not fit existing ways of ordering phenomena. The changes that result therefore require "putting on a different kind of thinking-cap", one that renders the anomalous lawlike but that, in the process, also transforms the order exhibited by some other phenomena, previously unproblematic.
>
> THOMAS KHUN
> *The Essential Tension*, p. xvii

5.1 Towards a New Paradigm in Macroeconomics

We opened this book by arguing that mainstream macroeconomics is in troubled methodological and explanatory waters. Throughout it we advocated that a possible way out from this quandary is a bottom-up approach: let us start from the analysis of the behaviour of heterogeneous constitutive elements (defined in terms of simple, observation-based behavioural rules) and their local interactions, and allow for the possibility that interaction nodes and individual rules change in time (adaptation). At the next meso-level, statistical regularities emerge that cannot be inferred from the primitives of individuals (self-emerging regularities). This emergent behaviour feeds back to the individual level (downward causation), but also produces aggregate regularities at the next hierarchical level. High-levels (macroeconomic) systems possess new and different properties than low-level (microeconomic) systems, like water has different properties from the atoms of hydrogen and oxygen that constitute it, as well as from ice and steam, and from the multicellular living organisms containing it. This approach allows each and every proposition to be falsified at micro, meso and macro levels and, de facto, it opposes to the mainstream axiomatic theory of economics, where microeconomic optimization is considered the rule for any rigorous scientific practice.

A paradigmatic example is the well-honoured model of racial segregation in cities proposed by Schelling (1978). He showed that individuals endowed with a relatively small preference for neighbours of one's own type organize themselves into high level of residential segregation through repeated housing decisions. Racial segregation emerges as an unintended aggregate consequence of individual purposive behaviours aimed at finding neighbours with slightly similar characteristics. Segregation is a property of a city as a whole (high-level system), not of the individuals and their primitives (low-level system). Another example which fits well with recent events is discussed by Thurner *et al.* (2009), who show that a rational attempt to control risk at a local level by individual lenders (for instance, by a bank which adjusts the leverage exposure of collateralized borrowers when the price of the asset used as collateral is dropping) can collectively induce a large instability in prices and involuntarily create more risk, because margin calls cause massive selling at just the wrong time. Fat tails and clustered volatility in price fluctuations emerge at the aggregate level even if all traders are value investors who individually wish to buy when prices fall, and *vice-versa*. Once again, the properties of the system as a whole can not be deduced from the primitive characteristics of the individuals, an argument we argue has general validity.

Similarly, levels and growth rates of aggregate output and employment, inflation, patterns of international trade, the impact of taxes on savings, the response of investments to interest rates and all other typical macroeconomic occurrences and laws (as, for instance, the ones associated to Phillips, Okun and Beveridge) are social phenomena that must be explained at a different level than microeconomic units.

As we have already emphasized in Chap. 1, an important mechanism responsible for the self-organizing macroscopic behaviour of a complex system is *autocatalyticity*, a property a simple unit possesses whenever the time variations of the quantities characterizing it are proportional (via stochastic factors) to their current values. Take the consequences of any adaptive behavioural rule you can think of for your model economy, and you will realize that you are thinking about autocatalytic agents. The performance of the whole is then dominated by the micro units which happen to experience the highest auto-catalytic stochastic growth rate, rather than by the behaviour of a typical or *representative* element. In the presence of auto-catalytic processes, therefore, a small amount of individual heterogeneity in initial conditions invalidates any dynamic description of the system in terms of its average.

Regulators working in primary organizations have at last recognized that a massive failure in realizing this plain fact is a key determinant of the recent financial turmoil; that a macroeconomic system in general – and the financial system in particular – is in its essence a network, with nodes defined by agents and links defined by the contractual obligations among them; that systemic risk in such a network is endogenous, as it depends on the interactive collective behaviour of financial institutions and market operators (Cecchetti *et al.*, 2009; Haldane, 2009; Papademos, 2009).

All this requires a new methodological approach and new tools. Complexity is the new paradigm for building macroeconomic models. Agent-based computational techniques are a natural device to analyze the phenomena emerging from the complex gathering of a multitude of interacting purposive agents, whose actions are aimed at satisfying individual needs and attaining individual objectives (Judd and Tesfatsion, 2006).

In a complex economy, since the consequences of individual choices depend on what all the others are autonomously doing, people take actions into an environment characterized by radical or endogenous uncertainty. The aggregate outcomes emerging from their continuous and asynchronous localized interactions are almost incomprehensible at an individual level. In spite of this, modern market economies display a reasonably coordinated state of affairs most of the time – say, within few percentage points from full-employment, and without persistent pathological shortages or surpluses of goods – unexpectedly punctuated by deep crisis. Borrowing a concept developed by Axel Leijonhufvud (1981, 2009), it is as if the system normally operates inside a *corridor* of stability – where even large shocks are absorbed without excessive casualties – to be sometimes pushed outside it along a ruinous path by apparently insignificant flips.[53] In other terms, the macroeconomy is characterized both by a substantial resilience and a deep fragility.

In addition to the and results we have discussed so far, this approach opens the way to some fundamental theoretical and policy questions that future research must seriously address, regarding how built-in feedback mechanisms operates in a complex economy, and how government interventions should interact with them to prevent future departures from the corridor. In the remaining of this section we discuss three of them.

5.2 Coordination in Asynchronous Markets

In a modern system of manufacturing, production firms are interrelated by a nexus of contractual and delivering arrangements, since each firm uses specialized goods and services that are produced by other firms in the system. Even if at an individual level production functions are convex, in the aggregate the economy can display *parallel scale economies* (Leijonhufvud, 1986) as soon as the system is sufficiently coordinated. Delays or failures in the delivering of just one input or obligation, however, can easily cascade through the whole interrelated system, potentially triggering coordination failures on a grand scale.

---

[53] In the U.S., the burst of the dot.com bubble on Wall Street in 2000 caused a loss in real GDP of around 1%. Contrast it with the currently estimated 8% loss associated to defaults in subprime mortgages, a tiny fraction of the market for loans.

In such a world, agents face endogenous uncertainty, that is uncertainty generated by their own actions. As shown by Chichilnisky (1999), in the presence of endogenous uncertainty markets are incomplete by definition, and no matter how many state-contingent securities are added into an Arrow-Debreu general equilibrium framework, Pareto efficient allocations cannot be reached. Markets cannot simultaneously hedge one another, given that even a Walrasian auctioneer cannot simultaneously determine the market-clearing contingent prices for a commodity and for the options aimed at hedging positions on that commodity. To understand why, suppose the auctioneer announces simultaneously market-clearing prices for all states and time periods. Futures contracts are in that case useless in allocating risk, as there is no price uncertainty left to hedge. In order to solve the problem, markets must be instead organized according to a sequenced order, so that the uncertainty on the states belonging to different logical classes – or *layers* – can be solved sequentially. Briefly, markets must clear according to a time hierarchy, with low-frequency markets receiving price and quantity signals from high-frequency ones.

In fact, this is the way markets are normally organized:

> Consider the simple case of bread. The wheat market clears annually. The inventory is drawn monthly. It can be hedged with three month futures contracts. Bakers rent their shops on five years contracts. Rental contracts are adjusted yearly, contingent on the price level. Bakers own their equipment in perpetuity, but borrow on three year notes to buy it. The commercial note markets clear hourly. Equipment orders take six months to produce. The used equipment market is thin; its transactions are episodic and few. Bakery employees are hired weekly. Bread is baked and consumed daily. (Arthur De Vany, 1996, p. 325)

Each market possesses its own frequency, which is dictated by the technological characteristics of the good or service exchanged (production period, durability, and so on), the bids and asks arrival rates, liquidity and the depth of the demand and supply processes. The aggregate activity thus emerges from the combination of markets operating at different frequencies and from their interrelations. When the rhythms in consumption and production in hierarchical organized markets gain systemic coherence, the economy can grow along a coordinated balanced path. The banking sector plays a crucial role in the process, as it provides liquidity means and maturity transformation services which allow firms and households to hold in their balance sheets credit assets and liabilities expiring at different settlement dates in different markets.

Of course, systemic coordination failures may occur if, for whatever reason, frequencies stop to support one another, and if displacements in one market propagate through the economy. The chronicle of the 2007–2009 global crisis is a case in point. An increase of subprime mortgage defaults (a market where contracts last ten to thirty years, and payments are made monthly) which started in February 2007 caused a prolonged decline in asset-backed securities (ABS) and credit default swaps (CDS) indices (whose market clears hourly); the decrease in ABS and CDS indices caused in turn a series of write-downs in commercial and investment banks' balance sheets (an information market which opens every three months); uncertainties on the consistency of potential losses in intermediaries' books triggered by the default of a primary investment bank dried-up liquidity on the inter-bank market (which clears daily); the generalized deleveraging process provoked a substantial restriction of lending to the private sector, which generated a displacement in the trade-credit market (on which payments occurs on 3-month notes). In general, the propagation process depends on which market is initially affected: shocks to high-frequency markets will be immediately transmitted but slowly propagated through the hierarchically organized multi-market structure, while shocks to low-frequency markets can remain for long cornered into a small portion of the aggregate economy before the transmission mechanism gains momentum, and their effects become systemic.

This modelling approach entails both positive and normative interesting research questions. Some of them can be borrowed from a small but inspiring literature devoted by economic geographers to the study of the spatial and temporal synchronization of periodic markets in rural areas (Hill and Smith, 1972; Symanski and Webber, 1974), that can be suitably adapted to proper macroeconomic analysis.

From a positive viewpoint, the key point is that of generating and assessing the properties of macro systems characterized by asynchronous interrelated markets. Several distinct topics worth exploring can be suggested. How does the right frequency of each market depends on the distribution and evolution of preferences and technologies of the agents operating in it, as well as on the market institutions organizing their transactions? How is information created and transmitted among markets operating at different frequencies? How can coordination be achieved by the emergence of an array of contractual arrangements forcing coherence among settlement dates in different markets? How are aggregate and idiosyncratic shocks propagated through the system? Is there a trade-off between resilience and fragility of the whole system in correspondence of alternative hierarchical market organizations?

Moving from this ground, the availability of a computational agent-based laboratory would allow to address additional normative questions. What sort of institutional arrangements – for instance, in terms of market microstructures, or imposed periodization – should be devised to coordinate decentralized actions in this interrelated system? In order to let the system maintain the coherence of market frequencies when serious displacements threaten to trigger a systemic crisis, should the supply of liquidity and market depth by public intervention be generalized or limited to selected markets? Can new contractual arrangements or new markets be designed and implemented, so that aggregate coordination is guaranteed?

5.3 Networks

Networks are the main subject of a rapidly growing literature which applies the conceptual and analytical tools already developed in sociology, computer science and physics to economics and/or provides new notions and methods to be applied specifically to economic phenomena.[54] Among them, the complex pattern of credit relationships is a natural research issue to be dealt with by means of network analysis, as it is straightforward to think of agents as nodes and of debt contracts as links in a credit network.

There are indeed influential examples of network analysis applied to credit networks. The most famous one is probably the model of financial contagion developed by Allen and Gale (2000) to explore the spreading of financial distress in the network of interbank relations. In this case, however, the networks considered are too simple and unrealistic as they consist of few nodes organized in canonical forms.[55] A related line of research (Boissay, 2006; Battiston *et al.* 2007) focuses on the network of trade-credit relationships within the corporate sector, i.e. among suppliers of intermediate goods and producers of final goods along a "supply chain". While these two strands of literature analyze specific credit relationships (among banks on the interbank market, and among firms along the supply chain), in our view there is a long way to go before reaching a comprehensive and satisfactory network model of credit relationships, since at least three features of a credit network must be reproduced in a model.

First and foremost, credit and credit networks are pervasive, so that a general and "encompassing" framework is needed. Agents are linked by *inside* credit – i.e. credit relationships connecting agents belonging to different layers of the same class of agents – and *outside* credit – i.e. credit relationships connecting agents belonging to different classes. Typical instances of inside credit are the interbank lending/borrowing relationships (within the banking industry) and the links between suppliers of intermediate goods and producers of final goods (within the corporate sector). As said above, in modern manufacturing firms are connected by a nexus of contractual arrangements, since each firm uses goods and services that are produced by other firms. The supplier (upstream firm), however, is not only the starting point of the supply chain but also the lender in a trade-credit relationship. The producer (downstream firm) correspondingly is not only the ending point of the supply chain but also the borrower in a trade credit relationship. The most straightforward example of outside credit, on the other hand, is the lending/borrowing relationship between a bank and a firm (or a household) on the market for bank loans (mortages).[56]

Second, networks are continuously changing. Their topological structure, in fact, is evolving over time due to the disruption of previous relationships and the formation of new ones. This is the consequence, in turn, of the choice of the partner in a relationship: old partners are abandoned and new ones are embraced.

---

[54] Recent books by Jackson (2008), Vega-Redondo (2007) and Goyal (2007) describe the frontier of research on economic networks. Caldarelli (2007) analyzes networks from the physicist's point of view. His book presents plenty of applications to different fields, economics being only one of them.

[55] A remarkable body of literature has developed from these premises (Freixas *et al.*, 2000; Furfine, 2003; Boss *et al.*, 2004; Iori *et al.*, 2006; Nier *et al.*, 2007).

[56] Battiston *et al.* (2007) and Delli Gatti *et al.* (2009) are examples of the type of analysis of credit network we have in mind.

Jackson (2005) distinguishes between a random graph approach to network evolution, borrowed from physics, and the game theoretic approach specifically designed to deal with economic networks. The former is, in a sense, "mechanical": network formation is purely stochastic or the product of an ad hoc algorithm. The latter focuses on "equilibrium" networks, where links are formed as a consequence of cost-benefit analysis on the part of self-interested agents.

As a useful approximation to real world network evolution, we argue for an approach which is in a sense half-way between the two: the choice of the preferred partner allocates links to nodes as a consequence of the search for the "best bargain" within the limits of an environment characterized by fundamental uncertainty. In every period, an agent in search of a partner in a transaction – a customer in search of a supplier, a firm in search of a bank – chooses the partner who offers the best terms, for instance she who posts the minimum price/interest rate, in a randomly selected subset of agents. Transaction costs in fact limit the search for a new partner to a neighbourhood of available partners. If the minimum price is lower than the price the agent paid to the old partner, she will switch to the new partner, otherwise she will stick to the old one. The number of links connecting the nodes, therefore, changes over time so that the topology of the network is also in a process of continuous evolution.

The execution of standard economic tasks – production, consumption, lending and borrowing – by each agent on each market occurs at a different time scale with respect to the choice of the partner. In other words, routine economic activity and the choice of the partner are organized according to a sequenced order, or time hierarchy. The choice of the partner is a low-frequency phenomenon while price and quantity determination is a high-frequency one. Of course the two are intertwined. Economic incentives are crucial – albeit not unique – in the choice of the partner and therefore in network formation.

Third, credit networks are fragile and vulnerable. In a financing hierarchy perspective, the scale of activity of each agent is constrained by a measure of her financial robustness, for instance her net worth. Changes in net worth of an agent, say borrower A, brings about changes in the same direction of agents, say lenders B and C, linked to A in a credit relationship. An unexpected shock to A's net worth, if large enough, may impair the ability of the borrower to fulfil debt commitments and may lead to bankruptcy.

The bankruptcy of a borrower would be irrelevant if, so to speak, the agent were an "island" or the network were fragmented in many relatively small and independent sub-networks. In a dense network, on the contrary, bankruptcy will not be an isolated and therefore insignificant phenomenon. The bankruptcy of a producer of final goods may bring about the default of the suppliers whom the producer interacts with along the supply chain. Moreover non-performing loans affect the net worth of banks, which can also go bankrupt. If they manage to survive, they will react to the deterioration of borrowers' financial conditions increasing the interest rate. The interest rate hike leads to more bankruptcies and eventually to a bankruptcy chain.

Establishing several credit relationships allows an agent to diversify the risk of a loss if the agent is hit by a negative shock, but it also entails the propagation of financial distress to connected agents, i.e. financial contagion in the wording of Allen and Gale. In this context, in principle one cannot rule out the risk of a systemic crisis, i.e. the diffusion and amplification of financial distress until the collapse of the financial system. In other words, as connectivity increases, a trade off emerges between individual risk – which decreases because of risk sharing – and systemic risk – which increases due to the amplification of financial distress. Therefore the relationship between connectivity and systemic risk is not monotonically decreasing as in Allen and Gale, but – at least under certain circumstances – it may be non monotonic (Battiston *et al.*, 2010).

Risk sharing, distress propagation and bankruptcy cascade can be conceived of in the most general terms as externalities. In case of a negative shock to an agent, these effects impose additional costs to the other nodes in the neighbourhood. Risk sharing however by itself is a benign externality. In the absence of the other effects, it will gently lead the probability of individual bankruptcy and of a systemic crisis to zero as the connectivity increases. On the contrary distress propagation and the bankruptcy cascade effect are malign externalities. They may amplify the effect of the initial shock and lead to a full fledged systemic crisis if they more than offset risk sharing.

The policy implications of this approach are obvious and far reaching. First of all, once the structure of the network has been analyzed and measured empirically (in terms of distance between nodes, diameter and average path length, presence of clusters and subgroups and so on), one could devise early warnings of a systemic crisis. Second, policy measures could be adopted to steer the structure of the network in a safer direction in case financial fragility and vulnerability become "excessive". For example, the heated discussion on the fact that some financial institutions are – or have become – "too big" and/or "too interconnected" to fail can be interpreted in network terms. A policy proposal to break up financial conglomerates may be grounded on the notion that clusters or "hubs" in the credit network carry a higher risk of contagion. The rationale behind a proposal to reintroduce barriers among different segments of the financing industry (for instance, by means of an updated version of the Glass-Steagall act) may be the need to reduce the connectivity of the network in order to attenuate the financial amplification mechanism described above.

5.4 Monetary Policy

As a natural extension of the arguments raised so far, the third item of the research agenda for complex macroeconomics we propose focuses on monetary policy. According to the general consensus, a central bank must perform three different tasks: *i*) it must provide a "nominal anchor" to the monetary unit used to sign contracts, to quote prices and to keep accounts, with the aim to control inflation and inflation expectations; *ii*) it must ensure that such an obligation is managed at minimum cost in terms of output fluctuations; *iii*) it must promote a secure and efficient payment system to prevent financial collapses and sudden shortages of means of payments. Standard macroeconomic monetary models insert tasks *i*)–*ii*) into a rational-expectation general-equilibrium framework to obtain optimally designed policies (Clarida *et al.*, 1999), while task *iii*) is simply ignored on the presumption of efficient markets and perfect arbitrage. The recent global financial crisis has dramatically proved how much wrong and misleading these assumptions could be.

In the complex adaptive macroeconomic system we are here depicting, endogenous uncertainty affects both the public *and* policy-makers, and the very notions of rational expectations and rational learning are meaningless. In the absence of a Walrasian auctioneer, individual agents can fail to coordinate their choices, and macro-financial instabilities materialize as a marker of such failures. Traditional monetary policy (tasks *i*–*ii*) and the promotion of stability in the financial system (task *iii*) – including the general provision of liquidity to financial institutions and other unconventional policies in the wake of a financial crisis – are thus interlinked and must be devised inside a unitary framework. Several interesting research questions arise from this approach.

A promising approach is the one rooted into the long tradition that goes back to the idea of a *natural rate of interest* elaborated by Knut Wicksell (1898) and the notion of *forced saving* developed by the Austrian school in the 1930s. Simply stated, the point is as follows. Suppose the economy possesses a real interest rate consistent with full employment and stable prices (and consistent private expectations thereof), and call it *natural*. In a world of radical uncertainty, a central bank which aims to peg the interest rate cannot know for sure where the natural rate is at any particular point in time, [57] and a discrepancy between the natural and the market rates can easily occur and be maintained for quite long. When the market rate is lower than its natural counterpart, entrepreneurs are encouraged to borrow from banks to undertake investments that will add to the supply of consumption goods in the future. However, that same discrepancy implies that consumers are not willing to sacrifice current consumption for future consumption (that is to save) at the rate expected by entrepreneurs to make their investments profitable. As a result, an intertemporal coordination failure between saving and investment emerges due to a wrong market signal: the economy builds up a stock of capital in excess to what is needed. Notice also that such a process can continue without overall price inflation if the economy is growing, and the rate of growth of available nominal money does not exceed that of the demand for real balances. The recent history of the U.S. and other industrialized economies – marked by exceptionally low interest rates, massive capital inflows from China and oil-producing countries, decreasing households' saving rates and a spectacular accumulation of office buildings, houses and excess productive capacity – can be interpreted along

---

[57] Not to talk of the possibility, suggested by Keynes in his *General Theory*, that the economy possesses multiple natural rates, many of which compatible with involuntary unemployment.

these lines. Mostly valuable for the issue we are dealing with, the grouping of large cumulating financial imbalances and of missing (CPI) inflation has shown that the practice of *inflation targeting* followed by many central banks around the world not only has failed to engineer financial stability as a by-product,[58] but in fact it has actively contributed to create asset-price bubbles (Leijonhufvud, 2007).

Once again, the crucial point is that saving-investment imbalances are emerging properties of a macroeconomic system composed of heterogeneous interacting units, and cannot be deduced from the primitive characteristics of a representative agent. As we abandon rational expectations, one must ask how monetary policy must be conducted to prevent an economy from sliding along a cumulative destabilizing path characterized by increasing financial instability. The lessons for monetary policy marvellously summarized by Howitt (2006) are a natural starting point for new research along a new paradigm. In particular, agent-based explorations of how adaptive heterogeneous mechanisms of expectation formation interact with different assumptions on how prices and quantities adjust in real time can shed additional light on the viability of alternative interest rate rules in anchoring inflation expectations, or in solving intertemporal coordination failures.[59]

A second strand of issues arises naturally as soon as one starts to think how monetary policies aimed at addressing tasks *i*) to *iii*) should be designed and implemented in the presence of endogenous waves of optimism and pessimism, that is what Keynes called *animal spirits*. For a couple of examples to be interpreted as a starting point for additional explorations, see De Grauwe (2009), who discusses a simple New-Keynesian model in which reinforcement learning mechanisms can generate correlations in beliefs, with interesting implications on the role of monetary policy in stabilizing output fluctuations; and Canzian *et al.* (2009), who insert a social contagion mechanism inside a dynamic IS-LM model to provide an agent-based description of the behavioural traits contained in Keynes' original description of the business cycle (Chap. 22 of the *General Theory*).

Finally, it could be interesting to extend the analysis put forth in Delli Gatti *et al.* (2005b), where some issues on the *rules-vs-discretion* debate are discussed in a fully decentralized macroeconomic agent-based model, where the learning processes of the central bank are mimicked by means of a genetic algorithm. In particular, such a framework could be usefully employed in evaluating alternative proposals on new macroprudential arrangements, or innovative feedback adaptive rules as the "Taylor rule for capital adequacy" recently proposed by Ingves (2009).

[58] In a previous life, Governor Bernanke made use of a New-Keynesian DSGE framework to ask himself whether central bankers should respond to movements in asset prices, and the answer he gave is negative: "Changes in asset prices should affect monetary policy only to the extent that they affect the central bank's forecast of inflation. To a first approximation, once the predictive content of asset prices for inflation has been accounted for, there should be no additional response of monetary policy to asset-price fluctuations" (Bernanke and Gertler, 2001, p. 253). Notice, incidentally, that the same conclusion is still sustained by recent research (conducted, needless to say, by means of a structural DSGE model) at the IMF (International Monetary Fund, 2009).

[59] On these points, see also Anufriev *et al.* (2009).

References

Ackerman, F. (2002) Still dead after all these years: interpreting the failure of general equilibrium theory, *Journal of Economic Methodology*, **9**:119–139.

Alchian, A. (1950) Uncertainty, evolution and economic theory, *Journal of Political Economy*, **58**:211–221.

Allen, F. and Gale, D. (2001) Financial contagion, *Journal of Political Economy*, **108**:1–33.

Amaral, L., Buldyrev, S., Havlin, S., Leschhorn, H., Maas, P., Salinger, M., Stanley, E. and Stanley, M. (1997) Scaling behavior in Economics: I. Empirical results for company growth, *Journal de Physique*, **7**:621–633.

Anderson, P. (1972) More is different, *Science*, **177**:393–396.

Anderson, P. (1997) Some thoughts about distribution in economics, in Arthur, B., Dulrauf, S. and Lane, D. (eds), *The Economy as an Evolving Adaptive System II*. Reading: Addison-Wesley.

Anufriev, M., Assenza, T., Hommes, C. and Massaro, D. (2009) Interest rate rules and macroeconomic stability under heterogeneous expectations, Cendef, University of Amsterdam, mimeo.

Aoki, M. (1996) New Approaches to Macroeconomic Modeling: Evolutionary Stochastic Dynamics, Multiple Equilibria, and Externalities as Field Effects. Cambridge, Cambridge University Press.

Aoki, M. (2002) Modeling Aggregate Behavior and Fluctuations in Economics. Cambridge, Cambridge University Press.

Aoki, M. and Yoshikawa, H. (2007) Non-self-averaging in macroeconomics models: a criticism of modern micro-founded macroeconomics, *RIETI Discussion paper series*, 07-E-057.

Ariely, D., Loewenstein, G. and Prelec, D. (2003) "Coherent arbitrariness": stable demand curves without stable preferences, *Quarterly Journal of Economics*, **118**:73–105.

Arrow, K. (1959) *Social choice and individual values*. New York, Wiley.

Arrow, K. (1964) The role of securities in the optimal allocation of risk-bearing, *Review of Economic Studies*, **31**:91–96.

Arrow, K. (1971) A utilitarian approach to the concept of equality in public expenditures, *Quarterly Journal of Economics*, **85**:409–415.

Arrow, K. and Debreu, G.(1954) The existence of an equilibrium for a competitive economy, *Econometrica*, **22**:265–290.

Arthur, B. (1992) Learning and adaptation in the economy, *Santa Fe Institute Paper 92-07-038*.

Arthur, B. (2006) Out-of-equilibrium economics and agent-based modelling, in Judd, K. and Tesfatsion, L. (eds.), *Handbook of Computational Economics 2*. Amsterdam, North Holland.

Arthur, B., Durlauf, S. and Lane, D. (eds.) (1997) *The economy as an evolving complex system II*. Reading, Addison-Wesley.

Axelrod, R. (1997) Advancing the art of simulation in the social sciences. In: Conte, R., Hegselmann, R., Terna, P. (eds). *Simulating Social Phenomena.* Berlin, Springer: 21–40.

Axtell, R. (2000) Why agents? On the varied motivations for agent computing in the social sciences. Center on Social and Economic Dynamics, *Working Paper 17.*

Axtell, R. (2001) Zipf 's distribution of US firms sizes, *Sciences*, **293**:1818–1820.

Axtell, R., Axelrdod, R., Epstein, J.M., and Cohen, M.D. (1996) Aligning simulation models: a case study and results, *Computational and Mathematical Organization Theory*, **1**:123–141.

Bak, P. (1997) *How nature works*. Oxford, Oxford University Press.

Barone, E. (1908) Il Ministro della produzione nello Stato collettivista, *Giornale degli Economisti.*

Barro, R. (1991) Economic Growth in a cross section of countries, *Quarterly Journal of Economics*, **106**:407–444.

Barro, R. (2006) Rare disaster and asset prices in the twentieth century, *Quarterly Journal of Economics*, **121**:823–866.

Batten, D. (2000) Discovering artificial economics: how agents learn and economies evolve. Boulder, CO, Westview Press.

Battiston, S., Delli Gatti, D., Gallegati, M., Greenwald, B. and Stiglitz, J. (2007) Credit chains and bankruptcies avalanches in supply networks, *Journal of Economic Dynamics and Control*, **31**:2061–2084.

Battiston, S., Delli Gatti, D., Gallegati, M., Greenwald, B. and Stiglitz, J. (2010) Liaisons Dangereuses: Increasing Connectivity, Risk Sharing and Systemic Risk, mimeo.

Becker, G. (1976) *The Economic Approach to Human Behavior*. Chicago, University of Chicago Press.

Beinhocker, E. (2006) The Origin of Wealth. Evolution, Complexity, and the Radical Remaking of Economics. Boston, Harvard Business School Press.

Bénabou, R. (1996) Heterogeneity, stratification and growth: macroeconomic implications of community structure and school finance, *American Economic Review*, **86**:584–609.

Bergstrom, T. (2001) Evolution of social behavior: individual and group selection models, *Economic Working paper series*, University of California at Santa Barbara.

Bernanke, B. and Gertler, M. (1989) Financial fragility and economic performance, *Quarterly Journal of Economics*, **105**:87–114.

Bernanke, B. and Gertler, M. (1990) Agency costs, net worth, and business fluctuations, *American Economic Review*, **79**:14–31.

Bernanke, B. and Gertler, M. (2001) Should central banks respond to movements in asset prices, *American Economic Review*, **91**:253–257.

Bewely, T. (1999) *Why wages don't fall during recessions*. Cambridge, Harvard University Press.

Bhaskar, V., Machin, S. and Reid, G. (1993) Price and quantity adjustment over the business cycle: evidence from survey data, *Oxford Economic Paper*, **45:**257–268.

Bianchi, C., Cirillo, P., Gallegati, M., and Vagliasindi, P. (2007) Validation in agent-based models: an investigation on the CATS model, *Journal of Economic Behaviour and Organization*, **67**:947–964.

Bianchi, C., Cirillo, P., Gallegati, M., and Vagliasindi, P. (2008) Validating and calibrating ACE models: a case study, *Computational Economics,* **30**:245–264.

Blanchard, O. (2008) The state of macro, *NBER Working Paper* No. 14259.

Blanchard, O. and Kyiotaki, N. (1987) Monopolistic competition and the effects of aggregate demand, *American Economic Review*, **77**:647–666.

Boissay, F. (2006) Credit chains and the propagation of financial distress, European Central Bank, Working Paper No. 573.

Boss M., Elsinger H., Summer, M. and Thurner, S. (2004) Network topology of the interbank market, *Quantitative Finance*, **4**:677–84.

Bottazzi, G., and A. Secchi (2005) Explaining the distribution of firm growth rates, *Rand Journal of Economics*, **37**:234–263.

Bowles, S. (1998) Endogenous preferences: the cultural consequences of markets and other economic institutions, *Journal of Economic Literature*, **36**:75–111.

Brock, W.A. (1999) Scaling in economics: a reader's guide, *Industrial and Corporate Change*, **8**:409–446.

Brock, W.A. and Durlauf, S.N. (2001) Discrete choice with social interactions, *Review of Economic Studies*, **68**:235–260.

Caballero, R. (1992) A fallacy of composition, *American Economic Review*, **82**:1279–1292.

Caldarelli, G. (2007) *Scale-free Networks*. Oxford, Oxford University Press.

Caldwell, B. (1993) *The Philosophy and Methodology of Economics*, vols I–III. Aldershot, Edward Elgar.

Campbell, C. and Kamlani, K. (1997) The reasons for wage rigidity: evidence from a survey of firms, *Quarterly Journal of Economics*, **112**:759–789.

Canning, D., Amaral, L., Lee, Y., Meyer, M. And Stanley, E. (1998) Scaling the volatility of GDP growth rates, *Economic Letters*, **60**:335–341.

Canzian, G., Gaffeo, E. and Tamborini, R. (2009) Keynes in the computer laboratory. An agent-based model with MEC, MPC, LP, in Hernàndez, C., Posada, M. and Lòpez-Parades, A. (eds), *Artificial Economics. The Generative Method in Economics*. Berlin, Springer.

Carley, K. (1996) *Validating computational models, mimeo*. Carnegie Mellon University.

Carroll, C. (1997) Buffer-stock saving and the life cycle/permanent income hypothesis, *The Quarterly Journal of Economics*, **112**:1–55.

Carroll, C. and Kimball, S. (1996) On the concavity of the consumption function, *Econometrica*, **64**:981–992.

Cecchetti, S., Disyatat, P. and Kohler, M. (2009) Integrating financial stability: new models for a new challenge, Bank for International Settlements, mimeo.

Chari, V., Kohe, P. and McGrattan, E. (2002) Accounting for the Great Depression, *American Economic Review*, **92**:22–27.

Chichilnisky, G. (1999) Existence and optimality of a general equilibrium with endogenous uncertainty, in Chichilnisky, G. (ed.), *Markets, Information and Uncertainty*. Cambridge, Cambridge University Press.

Christiano, L., Eichenbaum, M. and Evans, C. (2005) Nominal rigidities and the dynamic effects of a shock to monetary policy, *Journal of Political Economy*, **113**:1–45.

Churchland, P. and Sejnowski, T. (1992) *The computational brain*. Cambridge, MIT Press.

Cirillo, P. (2009) About the distribution of wages in Italy, submitted.

Cirillo, P., and Hüsler, J. (2009) On the upper tail of Italian firms' size distribution, *Physica A: Statistical Mechanics and its applications*, **388**:1546–1554.

Clarida, R., Galì, J. and Gertler, M. (1999) The science of monetary policy: a New-Keynesian perspective, *Journal of Economic Literature*, **37**:1661–1707.

Clark, A. (1997) Being There. Putting Brain, Body, and World Together Again. Cambridge, MIT Press.

Clementi, F., Gallegati, M. and Kaniadakis, G. (2007) κ-generalized statistics in personal income distribution, *The European Physical Journal B*, **57**:187–193.

Clementi, F., Di Matteo, T., Gallegati, M. and Kaniadakis, G. (2008) The κ-generalized distribution: a new descriptive model for the size distribution of incomes, *Physica A: Statistical Mechanics and its Applications*, **387**:3201–3208.

Cogley, T. and Nason, J. (1995) Output dynamics in real-business-cycle models, *American Economic Review*, **85**:492–511.

Cohen, A.J. and Harcourt, G.C. (2003) *Capital theory*. Cheltenham, Edward Elgar.

Colander, D. (ed.) (1996) *Beyond microfoundation*. Cambridge, Cambridge University Press.

Colander, D. (ed.) (2006) *Post Walrasian Macro: Beyond the DSGE Model*. Cambridge, Cambridge University Press.

Cole, H.L., Mailath, G.J. and Postlewaite, A. (1992) Social norms, savings behavior, and growth, *Journal of Political Economy*, **100**:1092–1125.

Cooper, R. (1999) *Coordination games*. New York, Cambridge University Press.

Davis, J. (2006) The turn in economics and the turn in economic methodology, *Journal of Economic Methodology*, **14**:275–290.

Dawkins, R. (1976) *The Selfish Gene*. Oxford, Oxford University Press.

Deaton, A. (1991) Saving and liquidity constraints, *Econometrica*, **59**:1221–1248.

Debreu, G. (1959) *The Theory of Value*. New York, Wiley.

Debreu, G. (1974) Excess demand functions, *Journal of Mathematical Economics*, **1**:15–21.

De Grauwe, P. (2009) Top-down versus bottom-up macroeconomics, paper presented at the CESifo Conference "What's wrong with modern macroeconomics", Munich, 6–7 november 2009.

Delli Gatti, D., Di Guilmi, C., Gaffeo, E., Giulioni, G., Gallegati, M. and Palestrini, A. (2005) A new approach to business fluctuations: heterogeneous interacting agents, scaling laws and financial fragility, *Journal of Economic Behavior & Organization*, **56**:489–512.

Delli Gatti, D., Gaffeo, E., Gallegati, M. and Palestrini, A. (2005b) Monetary policy, complexity and learning, *New Mathematics and Natural Computation*, **1**:109–128.

Delli Gatti, D., Gaffeo, E., Gallegati, M., Giulioni, G. and Palestrini, A. (2008) *Emergent Macroeconomics. An Agent-Based Approach to Business Fluctuations*. Milan, Springer.

Delli Gatti, D., Gallegati M., Greenwald B., Russo A. and Stiglitz, J. (2009) Business fluctuations and bankruptcy avalanches in an evolving network economy, *Journal of Economic Interaction and Coordination*, **4**:195–212.

Denzau, A. and D. North (1994) Shared mental models: ideologies and institutions, *Kyklos*, **47**:3–31.

De Vany, A. (1996) Synchronizing markets, mutual information, and the price level: coordination in a non-general equilibrium world, in Vaz, D. and K. Velupillai (eds), *Inflation, Institutions and Information: Essays in Honour of Axel Leijonhufvud*. London, McMillan.

Dew, N., Sarasvathy, S.D. and Venkataraman, S. (2004) The economic implications of exaptation, *Journal of Evolutionary Economics*, **14**:69–84.

Dosi, G., Fagiolo, G. and Roventini, A. (2008a) The microfoundations of business cycles: an evolutionary, multi-agent model, *Journal of Evolutionary Economics*, **18**:413–432.

Dosi, G., Fagiolo, G. and Roventini, A. (2008b) Schumpeter meeting Keynes: A policy-friendly model of endogenous growth and business cycles, LEM Working Paper No. 2008/21.

Driffill, J. (2008) Macroeconomic theory and the global economic crises, mimeo, Birkbeck College.

Durlauf, S.N. (1993) Non-ergodic economic growth, *Review of economic studies*, **60**:349–366.

Durlauf, S.N. and Young, H.P. (2001) *Social Dynamics*. Cambridge, MIT Press.

Dutta, P. and Radner, R. (1999) Market selection and the profit-maximization hypothesis, *Review of Economic Studies*, **66**:769–798.

Embrechts, P., Mikosch, T., and Kluppelberg, C. (1997) *Modelling extremal events*. Berlin and New York, Springer.

Epstein, J. (1999) Agent-based computational models and generative social science, *Complexity*, **4**:41–60.

Epstein, J. (2006) Generative Social Science. Studies in Agent-based Computational Modeling. Princeton, Princeton University Press.

Epstein, J. and R. Axtell (1996) Growing Artificial Societies: Social Science from the Bottom Up. Cambridge, MIT Press.

Evans, G. and Honkapohja, S. (2001) *Learning and expectations in macroeconomics*. Cambridge, Princeton University Press.

Fagiolo, G., Moneta, A., and Windrum, P. (2008) A critical guide to empirical validation of agent-based models in economics: methodologies, procedures, and open problems, *Computational Economics*, **30**:195–226.

Fazzari, S. and Athey, M. (1989) Asymmetric information, financing constraints and investment, *Review of Economic and Statistics*, **69**:481–487.

Feller, W. (1957) An introduction to probability theory and its applications. New York, Wiley.

Ferber, J. (1999) Multi-Agent Systems: An Introduction to Artificial Intelligence. Addison-Wesley.

Flake, G. (1998) The computational beauty of nature: computer explorations of fractals, chaos, complex systems, and adaptation. Cambridge, MIT Press.

Foley, D. (1994) A statistical equilibrium theory of markets, *Journal of Economic Theory*, **62**:321–346.

Foley, D. (1996) Statistical equilibrium in economics: method, interpretation, and an example, in Petri, F. and Hahn, F. (eds.), *General equilibrium: problems and prospects*.

Forni, M. and Lippi, M. (1998) Aggregation and the Microfoundations of Dynamic Macroeconomics. Oxford, Clarendon Press.

Fox, D. (1989) Conditional multivariate calibration, *Communications in Statistics*, **18**:2311–2330.

Freixas, X., Parigi, B. and Rochet, J. (2000) Systemic risk, interbank relations and liquidity provision by the central bank, *Journal of Money, Credit and Banking*, **32**:611–38.

Friedman, M. (1953) The methodology of positive economics, in Frideman, M. (ed.), *Essays in Positive Economics*. Chicago, University of Chicago Press.

Fujiwara, Y. (2004) Zipf law in firms bankruptcy, *Physica A*, **337**:219–230.

Furfine, C. (2003) Interbank exposures: quantifying the risk of contagion, *Journal of Money, Credit and Banking*, **35**:111–28.

Gabaix, X., Gopikrishnan, P., Plerou, V., and Stanley, H.E. (2003) A theory of power law distributions in financial markets fluctuations, *Nature*, **423**:267–70.

Gaffeo, E., Catalano, M., Clementi, F., Delli Gatti, D., Gallegati, M. and Russo, A. (2007) Reflections on modern macroeconomics: can we travel along a safer road?, *Physica A*, **382**:89–97.

Gaffeo, E., Delli Gatti, D., Desiderio S. and Gallegati, M. (2008) Adaptive microfoundations for emergent macroeconomics, *Eastern Economic Journal*, **34**:441–463.

Gallegati, M. (1994) Composition Effect and Economic Fluctuations, *Economic Letters*, **44**:123–126.

Gallegati, M., Palestrini, A., Delli Gatti, D. and Scalas, E. (2006) Aggregation of heterogeneous interacting agents: the variant representative agent framework, *Journal of Economic Interaction and Coordination*, **1**:5–19.

Gallegati, M. and Richiardi, M. (2009) Agent-based modelling in economics and complexity, in Mayer, B. (ed.), *Encyclopedia of Complexity and System Science*. Springer.

Geroski, P. (1991) *Market dynamics and entry*. Oxford, Basil Blackwell.

Gilbert, N. and Troitzsch, K. (2005) *Simulation for the Social Scientist*. Milton Keynes, Open University Press.

Gilli, M., and Winker, P. (2003) A global optimization heuristic for estimating agent-based models, *Computational Statistics and Data Analysis*, **42**:299–312.

Glaeser, E., Sacerdote, B. and Scheinkman, J. (1996) Crime and social interactions, *Quarterly Journal of Economics*, **111**:507–548.

Glaeser, E., Dixit, J. and Green, D.P. (2002) Studying hate crime with internet: what makes racists advocate racial violence? *Journal of Social Issues*, **58**:177–194.

Gode, D.K. and Sunder, S. (1993) Allocative efficiency of markets with zero intelligence traders: market as a partial substitute for individual rationality, *Journal of Political Economy*, **101**:119–137.

Goodfriend, M. and King, R. (1997) The New Neoclassical synthesis and the role of monetary policy, *NBER Macroeconomics Annual*, **12**:231–283.

Gorman, W.M. (1953) Community preference fields, *Econometrica*, **21**:63–80.

Gould, S. (1996) Full House: The Spread of Excellence From Plato to Darwin. New York: Harmony Books.

Gourieroux, C., and Monfort, A. (1996) *Simulation-based econometric methods*. Oxford, Oxford University Press.

Goyal, S. (2007) *Connections*. Princeton, Princeton University Press.

Greenwald, B., Kohn, M. and Stiglitz, J. (1990) Financial market imperfections and productivity growth, *Journal of Economic Behavior and Organization*, **13**:321–345.

Greenwald, B. and Stiglitz, J. (1986) Externalities in economies with imperfect information and incomplete markets, *The Quarterly Journal of Economics*, **101**:229–264.

Greenwald, B. and Stiglitz, J. (1990) Macroeconomic models with equity and credit rationing, in Hubbard R. (eds.), *Information, capital markets and investment*. Chicago, Chicago University Press.

Grüne, L., Semmler, W. and Sieveking, M. (2005) Creditworthiness and thresholds in a credti market model with multiple equilibria, Economic Theory, 25:287–315.

Haldane, A. (2009) Why banks failed the stress test, speech given at the Marcus-Evans Conference on Stress-Testing, February.

Hall, B.E. (1987) The relationship between firm size and growth, *Journal of Industrial Economics*, **35**:583–606.

Härdle, W. and Kirman, A. (1995) Nonclassical demand. A model-free examination of price-quantity relations in the Marseille fish market, *Journal of Econometrics*, **67**:227–257.

von Hayek, F. (1978) New Studies in Philosophy, Politics and the History of Ideas. Chicago, Chicago University Press.

Head, A. (1995) Country size, aggregate fluctuations, and international risk sharing, *Canadian Journal of Economics*, **28**:1096–1119.

Hildebrand, W. and Kirman, A. (1988) *Equilibrium analysis*. North-Holland.

Hill, P. and Smith, R. (1972) The spatial and temporal synchronization of periodic markets: evidence from four emirates in northern Nigeria, *Economic Geography*, **48**:345–355.

Hodgson, G. (1993) The Mecca of Alfred Marshall, *Economic Journal*, **103**:406–415.

Hodgson, G. (2007) Meanings of methodological individualism, *Journal of Economic Methodology*, **14**:211–226.

Holland, J. (1988) The global economy as an adaptive system, in Anderson, P., Arrow, K. and Pines, D. (eds), *The Economy as an Evolving Complex System*. Redwood City, Addison-Wesley.

Holland, J. (1996) The rationality adaptive agents, in Arrow, K., Colombatto, E. Perlman, M. and Schmidt C. (eds), *The Rational Foundations of Economic Behavior*. New York, St. Martin's Press.

Howitt, P. (2006) Monetary policy and the limitations of economic knowledge, in Colander, D. (ed.), *Post Walrasian Macroeconomics*. Cambridge, Cambridge University Press.

Howitt, P., Kirman, A., Leijonhufvud, A., Mehrling, P. and Colander, D. (2008) Beyond DSGE models: toward an empirically based macroeconomics, *American Economic Review*, **98**:236–240.

Ijiri, Y. and Simon, H.A. (1977) *Skew distributions and the size of business firms*. Amsterdam: North Holland.

Ingves, S. (2009) The monetary policy landscape in a financial crisis, *BIS Review*, 41/2009.

International Monetary Fund (2009) Lessons for monetary policy from asset price fluctuations, *World Economic Outlook*, Chapter 3, October.

Iori, G., Jafarey, S. and Padilla, F. (2006) Systemic risk on the interbank market, *Journal of Economic Behaviour and Organization*, **61**:525–540.

Israel, G. (2005) The science of complexity: epistemological problems and perspectives, *Science in Context*, **18**:1–31.

Jackson, M. (2005) The economics of social networks, in Blundell, R., Newey, W. and Persson, T. (eds), *Proceedings of the 9th World Congress of the Econometric Society*. Cambridge, Cambridge University Press.

Jackson, M. (2008) *Social and Economics Networks*. Princeton, Princeton University Press.

Jaynes, E.T. (1957) Information theory and statistical mechanics, *Physics Review*, **106:**620–630.

Jennings, N., Sycara, K. and Wooldridge, M. (1998) A roadmap of agent research and development, *Autonomous Agents and Multi-agent Systems*, **1**:7–38.

Jorgenson, D., Lau, L.J. and Stoker, T.M. (1982) The transcendental logarithmic model of aggregate consumer behavior, in Basmann, R.L. and G. Rhodes (eds.), *Advances in Econometrics*, Vol. L. Greenwich, JAI Press.

Judd, K. and Tesfatsion, L. (2006) *Handbook of Computational Economics 2*. Amsterdam, North Holland.

Juselius, K. and Franchi, M. (2007) Taking a DSGE model to the data meaningfully, *Economics E-journal Discussion Paper*, 2007–6.

Kaldor, N. (1965) Capital accumulation and economic growth, in: Lutz, F.A., Hague, D.C. (eds). *The theory of capital. Proceedings of a Conference held by the International Economic Association*. London: MacMillan.

Kahneman, D. and Tversky, A. (1981) The framing of decisions and the psychology of choice, *Science*, **211:**453–458.

Kalejan, H.H. (1980) Aggregation and disaggregation of nonlinear equations, in: Kmenta, J. and Ramsey, J.B. (eds.), *Evaluation of econometrics models*. Academic, NewYork.

Kawasaki, S., McMillan J. and Zimmerman, K. (1982) Disequilibrium dynamics: an empirical study, *American Economic Review*, **72**:992–1004.

Keynes, J. (1921) *A Treatise on Probability*. London, McMillan.

Keynes, J. (1936) *The General Theory of Employment, Interest and Money*. New York, Harcourt, Brace and World.

Kirman, A. (1992) Whom or what does the representative individual represent?, *Journal of Economic Perspectives*, **6**:117–136.

Kirman, A. (1999) Interaction and markets, in Gallegati, M. and Kirman A. (eds), *Beyond the Representative Agent.* Cheltenham, Edward Elgar.

Kleijnen, J.P.C. (1995) Verification and validation of simulation models, *European Journal of Operational Research*, **82**:145–162.

Klevmarken, N.A. (1998) Statistical inference in microsimulation models: incorporating external information, *Working Paper* of Uppsala University, Department of Economics.

Knight, F. (1921) *Risk, Uncertainty and Profit*. Boston, Houghton Mifflin.

Kydland, F. and Prescott, E. (1982) Time to build and aggregate fluctuations, *Econometrica*, **50**:1345–1370.

Laidler, D. (1984) The "buffer stock" notion in monetary economics, *Economic Journal*, **94**:17–34.

Lavoie, D. (1989) Economic chaos or spontaneous order? Implication for political economy of the new view of science, *Cato Journal*, **8**:613–640.

Leibenstein, H. (1950) Bandwagon, snob, and veblen effects in the theory of consumers' demand, *Quarterly Journal of Economics*, **64**:183–207.

Leijonhufvud, A. (1981) *Information and Coordination*. Oxford, Oxford University Press.

Leijonhufvud, A. (1986) Capitalism and the factory system, in Langlois, R. (ed.), *Economics as a Process: Essays in the New Institutional Economics*. Cambridge, Cambridge University Press.

Leijonhufvud, A. (2006) Agent-based macro, in Judd, K. and Tesfatsion, L. (eds.), *Handbook of Computational Economics 2*. Amsterdam, North Holland.

Leijonhufvud, A. (2007) Monetary and financial stability, *CEPR Policy Insight*, No. 14.

Leijonhufvud, A. (2009) Out of the corridor: Keynes and the crisis, *Cambridge Journal of Economics*, **33**:741–757.

Lewbel, A. (1989) Exact aggregation and a representative consumer, *The Quarterly Journal of Economics*, **104**:621–633.

List, J. and Millimet, D. (2008) The market: catalyst for rationality and filter of irrationality, *The B.E. Journal of Economic Analysis & Policy*, Vol.8, Iss.1 (Frontiers), Article 47.

Long, J. and Plosser, C. (1983) Real business cycles, *Journal of Political Economy*, **91**:39–69.

Lucas, R. (1987) *Models of Business Cycles*. Oxford, Basil Blackwell.

Lucas, R. and Sargent, T. (1978) After Keynesian economics, in *After the Phillips Curve. Persistence of High Inflation and High Unemployment*, Federal Reserve Bank of Boston Conference Series No. 19. Boston, Federal Reserve Bank of Boston.

MacFadzean, D. and Tesfatsion, L. (1999) A C++ platform for the evolution of trade networks, *Computational Economics*.

Mandelbrot, B. (1960) The Pareto-Levy law and the distribution of income, *International Economic Review*, **1**:79–106.

Mantegna, R. and Stanley, E. (2000) *An introduction to econophysics*. Cambridge, England, Cambridge University Press.

Mantel, R. (1974) On the characterization of aggregate excess demand, *Journal of Economic Theory*, **7**:348–353.

Marks, R. (2007) Validating simulation models: a general framework and four applied examples, *Computational Economics*, **30**:265–290.

Marshall, A. (1961) *The Principles of Economics*, 9th edition. London: McMillan.

Mayr, E. (1988) Toward a New Philosophy of Biology – Observations of an Evolutionist. Cambridge, Harvard University Press.

Miller, J. and Page, S. (2007) Complex Adaptive Systems. An Introduction to Computational Models of Social Life. Princeton, Princeton University Press.

Minsky, M. (1986) *The Society of Mind*. New York, Simon and Schuster.
Mirowski, P. (1989) More Heat than Light. Economics as Social Physics, Physics as Nature's Economics. Cambridge, Cambridge University Press.
Nelson, R. and Winter, S. (1982) *An Evolutionary Theory of Economic Change*. Cambridge, Harvard University Press.
Nier, E., Yang, J., Yorulmazer, T. and Alentorn, A. (2007) Network models and financial stability, *Journal of Economic Dynamics and Control*, **31**:2033–2060.
Okuyama, K., Takayasu, H., and Takayasu, M. (1999) Zipf 's law in income distribution of companies, *Physica A*, **269:**125–131.
Papademos, L. (2009) Financial stability and macro-prudential supervision: objectives, instruments and the role of ECB, speech given at the "The ECB and its watchers XI" Conference, September.
Phelps, E. (1990) *Seven Schools of Macroeconomic Thought*. Oxford, Oxford University Press.
Pollack, R. (1976) Interdependent preferences, *American Economic Review*, **66**:309–320.
Prabhakar, M.D.N., Xie, M., Jiang, R. (2003) *Weibull models*. New York: Wiley.
Quandt, R.E. (1966) On the size distribution of firms, *American Economic Review*, **56**:416–432.
Ramsden, J. and Kiss-Haypal, G. (2000) Company size distribution in different countries. *Physica A*, **277**:220–227.
Rappaport, S. (1996) Abstraction and unrealistic assumptions in economics, *Journal of Economic Methodology*, **3**:215–236.
Reynard, E. (1979) A method for relating research spending to net profit, *Research Management*, **22**:12–14.
Richter, M. and Wong, K. (1999) Non-computability of competitive equilibrium, *Economic Theory*, **14**:1–28.
Richiardi, M., Leombruni, R., Saam, N.J. and Sonnessa, M. (2006) A common protocol for agent-based social simulation, *Journal of Artificial Societies and Social Simulation*, **9**.
Rios-Rull (1995) Models with Heterogeneous Agents, in Cooley, T. (ed.), *Frontiers of Business Cycles Research*. Princeton: Princeton University Press.
Rosser, B. (2001) Complex ecologic-economic dynamics and environmental policy, *Ecological Economics*, **37**:23–37.
Russo, A., Catalano, M., Gaffeo, E., Gallegati, M. and Napoletano, M. (2007) Industrial dynamics, fiscal policy and RD: evidence from a computational experiment, *Journal of Economic Behavior and Organization*, **64**:426–447.
Rust, J. (1998) Dealing with the complexity of economic calculations, in Durlauf, S. and Traub, J. (eds), *Limits to Knowledge in Economics*. New York: Addison-Wesley.
Saari, D. (1985) Iterative price mechanism, *Econometrica*, **53**:1117–1131.
Saari, D. and Simon, C. (1978) Effective price mechanism, *Econometrica*, **46**:1097–1125.
Sargent, T.J. (1998) Verification and validation in simulation models, *Proceedings of 1998 Winter Simulation Conference*, 52–64.
Savage, L. (1954) *The foundations of statistics*. New York, Wiley.
Saviotti, P. and Pyka, A. (2008) Product variety, competition and economic growth, *Journal of Evolutionary Economics*, **18**:323–347.
Schelling, T. (1978) *Micromotives and Macrobehavior*. New York, Norton.
Schubik, M. (1975) *The uses and methods of gaming*. Amsterdam, Elsevier.
Schumpeter, J. (1908) Das Wesen und der Hauptinhalt der theoretischen Nationalökonomie. Vien, Leipzig, Duncker & Humblot.
Shy, O. (2001) *The economics of network industries*. Cambridge, Cambridge University Press.
Simon, H.A. (1955) On a class of skew distribution functions, *Biometrika*, **42**:425–440.
Simon, H.A. (1987) Satisficing, in Eatwell, J., Milgate, M. and Newman, P. (eds), *The New Palgrave: A Dictionary of Economics*. New York, Wiley.
Simon, H.A. (1997) *Models of bounded rationality, vol. III*. Cambridge, MA, MIT Press.
Simon, H. (2000) Barriers and bounds to rationality, *Structural Change and Economic Dynamics*, **11**:243–253.

Smets, F. and Wouters, R. (2003) An estimated dynamic stochastic general equilibrium model of the Euro Area, *Journal of the European Economic Association*, **1**:1123–1175.

Solomon, S. (2007) The microscopic representation of complex macroscopic phenomena, mimeo, Hebrew University.

Sonnenschein, H. (1972) Market excess demand functions, *Econometrica*, **40**:549–563.

Sornette, D. (2000) Critical phenomena in natural sciences. Chaos, fractals, self organization and disorder: concepts and tools. Berlin, Springer.

Souleles, N. (1999) The response of household consumption to income tax refunds, *American Economic Review*, **89**:947–958.

Stanley, M., Amaral, L., Buldyrev, S., Havling, S., Leshorn, H., Maas, P., Salinger, M. and Stanley, E. (1996) Scaling behavior in the growth of companies, *Nature*, **379**:804–806.

Stiglitz, J. (1989) Financial markets and development, *Oxford Review of Economic Policy*, **5**:55–68.

Stiglitz, J. and Greenwald, B. (2003) *Towards a new paradigm in monetary economics*. Cambridge, CUP.

Stoker, T. (1984) Completeness, distribution restriction, and the form of aggregate function, *Econometrica*, **52**:887–907.

Subbotin, M.T. (1923) The law of frequency of error, *Mathematicheskii Sbornik*, **31**:296–301.

Sutton, J. (1997) Gibrat's legacy, *Journal of Economic Literature*, **35**:40–59.

Symanski, R. and Webber, M: (1974) Complex periodic market cycles, *Annals of the Association of American Geographers*, **64**:203–213.

Tesfatsion, L. (2002) Agent-based computational economics: growing economies from the bottom up, *Artificial life*, **8**:55–82.

Tesfatsion, L. (2005) Agent-based computational modelling and macroeconomics, *Staff general research papers*, Iowa State University, Department of Economics.

Tesfatsion, L. (2009) Website on Validation of ACE: http://www.econ.iastate.edu/tesfatsi/empvalid.htm

Thurner, S., Farmer, D. and Geanakoplos, J. (2009) Leverage causes fat tails clustered volatility, Santa Fe Institute, mimeo.

Togati, D. (2001) Keynes as the Einstein of economic theory, *History of Political Economy*, **33**:117–138.

Troitzsch, K. (2004) Validating simulation models, *Proceedings of the 18th European Simulation Multiconference*, 98–106.

Udhén (2001) Methogological Individualism. Background, History and Meaning. London, Routledge.

Vagliasindi, P., Romanelli, M. and Bianchi, C. (2003) Microsimulating the evolution of italian pension benefits: the role of retirement choices and lowest pensions indexing, *Labor*, **17**:139–73.

Vanberg, V. (2002) Rational choice vs. program-based behavior: alternative theoretical approaches and their relevance for the study of institutions, *Rationality and Society*, **14**:7–53.

Vanberg, V. (2004) The rationality postulate in economics: its ambiguity, its deficiency and its evolutionary alternative, *Journal of Economic Methodology*, **11**:1–29.

Veblen, T. (1899) *The Theory of the Leisure Class*. New York, The Viking Press.

Vega-Redondo, F. (2007) *Complex Social Networks*. Cambridge, Cambridge University Press.

Velupillai, K. (2000) *Computable Economics*. Oxford, Oxford University Press.

Velupillai, K. (2002) Effectivity and constructivity in economic theory, *Journal of Economic Behavior and Organization*, **49**:307–325.

Velupillai, K. (2005) A primer on the tools and concepts of computable economics, in Velupillai, K. (ed.), *Computability, Complexity and Constructivity in Economic Analysis*. Oxford, Blackwell.

Vriend, N. (1994) A new perspective on decentralized trade, *Economie Appliquée*, **47**:5–22.

Weisfeld, M. (2004) *The Object-Oriented Thought Process*. Indianapolis, Pearson Education.

Wicksell, K. (1898) *Interest and Prices* (translated by R. Kahn, London McMillan for the Royal Economic Society, 1936).

Winker, P. and Gilli, M. (2001) Indirect estimation of parameters of agent based models of financial markets, *Working Paper* presented at the 2001 International Conference on Computing in Economics and Finance of the Society for Computational Economics.

Witt, U. (1986) Firm's market behavior under imperfect information and economic natural selection, *Journal of Economic Behavior and Organization,* **7**:265–290.

Woodford, M., (2008) Convergence in macroeconomics: elements of the New Synthesis, *American Economic Journal: Macroeconomics*, **1**:267–279.

Wooldridge, M. (2002), *Introduction to Multi-Agent Systems*. New York, Wiley.

Zipf, G.K. (1932) Selective studies and the principle of relative frequency in language. Cambridge, Cambridge University Press.

Index

New Economic Window Series

Chatterjee A., Yarlagadda S., Chakrabarti B.K. (Eds.)
Econophysics of Wealth Distributions
2005, ISBN 978-88-470-0329-3

Salzano M., Kirman A.P. (Eds.)
Economics: Complex Windows
2005, ISBN 978-88-470-0279-1

Chatterjee A., Chakrabarti, B.K. (Eds.)
Econophysics of Stock and other Markets
2006, ISBN 978-88-470-0501-3

Salzano M., Colander D. (Eds.)
Complexity Hints for Economic Policy
2007, ISBN 978-88-470-0533-4

Chatterjee A., Chakrabarti, B.K. (Eds.)
Econophysics of Markets and Business Networks
2007, ISBN 978-88-470-0664-5

Gatti D., Gaffeo E., Gallegati M., Giulioni G., Palestrini A.
Emergent Macroeconomics. An Agent-Based Approach to Business Fluctuations
2008, ISBN 978-88-470-1561-6

Faggini M., Lux T. (Eds.)
Coping with the Complexity of Economics
2009, ISBN 978-88-470-1082-6

Basu B., Chakrabarti B.K., Chakravarty S.R., Gangopadhyay K. (Eds.)
Econophysics & Economics of Games, Social Choices and Quantitative Techniques
2010, ISBN 978-88-470-1500-5

Faggini M., Vinci C.P. (Eds.)
Decision Theory and Choices: a Complexity Approach
2010, ISBN 978-88-470-1777-1

Abergel F., Chakrabarti B.K., Chakraborti A., Mitra M. (Eds.)
Econophysics of Order-driven Markets
2011, ISBN 978-88-470-1765-8

Delli Gatti D., Desiderio S., Gaffeo E., Cirillo P., Gallegati, M.
Macroeconomics from the Bottom-up
2011, ISBN 978-88-470-1970-6

For further information, please visit the following link:
http://www.springer.com/series/9601

FSC
www.fsc.org
MIX
Papier | Fördert gute Waldnutzung
FSC® C083411

Kolibri 360 GmbH
Ferdinand-Jühlke-Straße 7
99095 Erfurt, Deutschland
produktsicherheit@kolibri360.de